Just How Married Do You Want To Be?

Practicing Oneness in Marriage

Jim & Sarah Sumner
Foreword by John and Kathy Burke

EasyRead Large

Copyright Page from the Original Book

InterVarsity Press
P.O. Box 1400, Downers Grove, IL 60515-1426
World Wide Web: www.ivpress.com
E-mail: email@ivpress.com

©2008 by Jim Sumner and Sarah Sumner

All rights reserved. No part of this book may be reproduced in any form without written permission from InterVarsity Press.

InterVarsity Press® is the book-publishing division of InterVarsity Christian Fellowship/USA®, a student movement active on campus at hundreds of universities, colleges and schools of nursing in the United States of America, and a member movement of the International Fellowship of Evangelical Students. For information about local and regional activities, write Public Relations Dept., InterVarsity Christian Fellowship/USA, 6400 Schroeder Rd., P.O. Box 7895, Madison, WI 53707-7895, or visit the IVCF website at <www.intervarsity.org>.

All Scripture quotations, unless otherwise indicated, are taken from the New American Standard Bible®, *copyright 1960, 1962, 1963, 1968, 1971, 1972, 1973, 1975, 1977, 1995 by The Lockman Foundation. Used by permission.*

Design: Janelle Rebel

Images: Punchstock

ISBN 978-0-8308-3393-1

Printed in the United States of America ∞

 InterVarsity Press is committed to protecting the environment and to the responsible use of natural resources. As a member of Green Press Initiative we use recycled paper whenever possible. To learn more about the Green Press Initiative, visit <www.greenpressinitiative.org>.

Library of Congress Cataloging-in-Publication Data

Sumner, Jim, 1956-
  Just how married do you want to be? : practicing oneness in marriage
  /Jim and Sarah Sumner.
      p. cm.
    Includes bibliographical references and index.
    ISBN 978-0-8308-3393-1 (pbk.: alk. paper)
    1. Marriage—Religious aspects—Christianity. 3. Patriarchy—Religious aspects—Christianity. I. Sumner, Sarah, 1963- II. Title.
BT706.S86 2008
248.8'44—dc22

                                                                                  2008017362

P 23 22 21 20 19 18 17 16 15 14 13 12 11 10 9 8 7 6 5 4 3 2 1
Y 27 26 25 24 23 22 21 20 19 18 17 16 15 14 13 12 11 10 09 08

TABLE OF CONTENTS

FOREWORD	vi
INTRODUCTION: Becoming One Flesh	x
1: AN UNLIKELY COUPLE	1
2: TWO POPULAR MODELS OF MARRIAGE	24
3: A DEEPER UNDERSTANDING OF HEADSHIP	47
4: A BIBLICAL MODEL OF MARRIAGE	73
5: PRACTICING ONENESS IN THE GRIND OF DAILY LIVING	90
6: RESOLVING CONFLICT	122
7: DEFINING EXPECTATIONS	152
8: HOT BUTTON ISSUES	176
9: BUILDING A CHRIST-CENTERED MARRIAGE	199
10: EVERY COUPLE'S NEED FOR CHRISTIAN COMMUNITY	224
ACKNOWLEDGMENTS	253
NOTES	258
BACK COVER MATERIAL	275

"We each read Sarah and Jim's book in one sitting ... and since then we have gone back and reread several passages that we found especially helpful. One of the things that we love about *Just How Married Do You Want to Be?* is that it contains profound biblical theology that is incredibly practical. We believe you will find this book to be an enjoyable read that has the potential to change your marriage."

GREG NETTLE, SENIOR PASTOR, AND **JULIE NETTLE,** WORSHIP LEADER, RIVERTREE CHRISTIAN CHURCH, MASSILON, OHIO

"Matching faithful, Christ-centered scriptural exposition with honest, down-to-earth sharing, the Sumners show how marriage minus role-play becomes relationally real. This is a truly health-giving read."

J.I. PACKER, AUTHOR, *KNOWING GOD*

"*Just How Married Do You Want to Be?* is the memoir of a marriage—riveting, honest, self-revelatory and full of evidences of the grace and mercy of Christ—and a reexamination of the meaning of headship in marriage. Readers will walk away from this book with a vivid memory of the fascinating courtship and marital journey of Jim and Sarah Sumner, and with important new insights related to a biblical theology of marriage. I highly recommend this book."

DR. DAVID P. GUSHEE, DISTINGUISHED UNIVERSITY PROFESSOR OF CHRISTIAN ETHICS, MCAFEE SCHOOL OF THEOLOGY, AND PRESIDENT, EVANGELICALS FOR HUMAN RIGHTS

"Sarah and Jim's book has theological depth, and is a great and timely teaching tool for changing the way people think about marriage, Christ and the church."

CHUCK COLSON, FOUNDER, PRISON FELLOWSHIP

"*Just How Married Do You Want to Be?* delivers the best of both worlds—an insightful, fresh, biblical framework for marriage along with real-world application. Jim and Sarah's straightforward honesty is compelling, raw and powerful. This is a great marriage resource not to simply read but to reflect on and study."

JUD WILHITE, SENIOR PASTOR, CENTRAL CHRISTIAN CHURCH, LAS VEGAS, AND AUTHOR OF *STRIPPED: UNCENSORED GRACE ON THE STRRTS OF VEGASS*

"Jim and Sarah Sumner have written perhaps the most honest marriage book we have ever read—an honesty born of the real-life pain and struggle of two people with very different backgrounds and personalities. The really good news is that they have looked straight into the heart of those differences and discovered that Jesus is the one who makes marriages work. Here is a marriage book without syrupy formulas or platitudes that tells us the truth that Jesus works through flawed vessels to create something beautiful."

FRANK JAMES, PRESIDENT, REFORMED THEOLOGICAL SEMINARY—ORLANDO, AND **CAROLYN JAMES,** AUTHOR OF *THE GOSPEL OF RUTH*

"'More than ever' is our response to Jim and Sarah's literary question, *Just How Married Do You Want to Be?*—and we're celebrating fifty years of practicing oneness!"

STUART AND JILL BRISCOE, AUTHORS AND SPEAKERS ON "TELLING THE TRUTH"

"Jim and Sarah Sumner's book provides a biblical model for marriage, enabling you to strengthen your relationship's foundation. They show you that marriage is a covenant and a commitment, not just feelings and emotions. They teach you how to get together on the vertical, so that things will go well on the horizontal. This emphasis on the primacy of the spiritual is refreshing."

BARRY C. BLACK, PH.D., CHAPLAIN, UNITED STATES SENATE

To our siblings, Becky, John and Debbie, because of their prayers for our marriage.

FOREWORD

Marriage is easy ... if you're a perfect person married to another perfect person! For the rest of us imperfect people, marriage feels a lot more like God's Gym. We all want health and fitness and loving strength, but as we soon realized after getting married nineteen years ago, this doesn't come without training and hard work. Most couples today put more effort into staying in shape physically than training to be a partner that can make love last.

Maybe to a large extent this is because we don't have a clear picture of what marriage looks like—what we're shooting for. We know what a ripped, toned physique looks like because it's plastered all over magazine covers, billboards and TV shows. But what does a strong, healthy, godly marriage look like? What's the image we can hold in our minds to motivate us to work and push hard to bring to life with our spouse?

In *Just How Married Do You Want to Be?* Jim and Sarah Sumner deliver a unique treasure: a truly biblical and mysterious, yet compelling and captivating picture of what God intends marriage to look like. Unfortunately, this treasure has been buried for centuries under arguments about roles of men and women, who leads in the home, and the meaning of a single word: *headship.* Sarah brings much needed biblical scholarship and insight that clear away the debris to unearth this valuable, God-given metaphor of marriage as one flesh. This thoroughly biblical view has been obscured and neglected far too long, but we believe it is the motivational picture every couple needs to put up in their gym of marriage to strive to achieve.

As Jim and Sarah say, marriage is not a commodity for couples to have or use. It's a holy relationship, not a product. Marriage is not meant to be consumed as a benefits package. Sadly, this mystery of "one flesh" is not understood by most couples, even among Christ followers. The truth is, even Christians often have more of a commodity mentality than a one-flesh mentality.

Whether you're already married, hopeful to be one day, or even if you'd opt for jail time over marriage right now due to the painful effects of a past relationship, Jim and Sarah will lead you into a fresh, inspiring understanding of what God had in mind when he said that two people would mysteriously become one. This mystery, which mirrors Christ's relationship to his church, will deepen not only your understanding of marriage but your understanding of God's passionate, loving commitment to you and your spouse as well.

With a biblical portrait of marriage in mind, Jim and Sarah take you into the raw reality of seeking to live out this one-flesh relationship. Sharing their own struggles and victories, they give fresh insight and practical ideas for living out oneness in matters like resolving conflict, dealing with letdowns and unmet expectations, as well as men's and women's unique temptations and struggles.

We have known Jim and Sarah for well over a decade now. We've worked alongside Sarah and quickly recognized her as a gifted teacher and theologian. We had the privilege of watching Sarah and Jim fall in love and get married, and over the years some things have never changed: their enthusiastic love for people, their raw authenticity, their unnerving vulnerability and their humble, passionate pursuit of God's will. That's the gift you'll receive in this invaluable book—theological insight mixed with gutsy realism and practical wisdom. You'll never view marriage the same way again!

John Burke, author, *No Perfect People Allowed* and *Soul Revolution,* and Kathy Burke, Gateway Church, Austin, Texas

INTRODUCTION

Becoming One Flesh

To participate in marriage is to be part of something holy. To be holy is to be whole. To be holy is to be attached to God. There's no such thing as secular matrimony; there's only holy matrimony.

To be holy also means to "be set apart." By God's design, marriage is set apart from every other type of human bond. Unlike the family bond between parents and children and siblings, marriage isn't grounded in biology. Marriage finds its basis in a spiritual covenant that is legitimized and ratified by God. When a couple is concerned about their holiness, they're concerned about the health of their marriage.

We've been married for almost twelve years, and we can honestly say that these have been seven of the happiest years of our whole lives! It's been hard, but it's been good because both of us have grown enormously. Our faith in God has grown, our marital love has grown, and each of us has grown as individuals. You see, we are in the process of becoming one flesh.

To become one flesh is to engage holistically in self-giving mutual love. To love is to be selfless. To love is to be Christlike. Frankly, neither one of us is good at this. We aren't good at being selfless, and we aren't good at being Christlike. Yet we're hopeful because we're learning to be both.

To say the same thing differently, we are being trained to be forgivers. Every time we forgive, we become more Christlike. We don't want to make excuses for each other, but neither do we want to harbor bitterness. We want to build our marriage on a bedrock of trust that allows us to be truthful with each other.

Without trust, couples can't be open with each other without sprinkling in half-truths. Way too many people end up hiding their real feelings from their spouse. Then as followers of Christ, they end up fighting spiritual battles all alone. Worst of all, some resign themselves eventually to a status quo mentality that tacitly declares, *This is just the way our marriage is.*

Jim and I don't want that. We refuse to settle for less than what the Bible says that God wants for our marriage.

Holy Matrimony

It was God who ordained the special union of husband and wife back in the Garden of Eden. Yet strikingly, God did not choose to create Adam and Eve as two married persons as such. In the opening stage of their life, Adam and Eve were both single. When Adam first saw Eve, he didn't call her "Wife"; he called her "Woman" (Genesis 2:23).[1]

The implication in Genesis is that marriage doesn't happen automatically in the natural course of things. It happens by means of a choice. A moral choice is made when a couple gets married.[2]

Many Christians today have forgotten this. How many believers have bought into the lie that says marriage and morality are unrelated? In twenty-first century culture, marriage is often seen as a promise that doesn't really have to be kept. It isn't that uncommon for couples in the church to fail to take seriously that together they have taken a vow. A wedding vow is a lifelong commitment to marriage "until death do us part."

Recently we were counseling a married Christian couple who no longer love each other. As the four of us conversed, the tension between the two of them mounted to a head. Suddenly the wife began to shriek, "I don't love him anymore! Our love is gone! That's why this marriage is over!"

We glanced at each other. Then I (Sarah) said to the wife, "You don't have to love each other to stay married. Marriage isn't built on love. Marriage is built on a covenant, a commitment. Your marriage isn't over until both of you give up on your commitment."

Jim added, "It's not about you *being* loved. It's about you learning *to* love."

Marriage is not a possession for people to "have." Holy matrimony is a holy relationship, not a commodity for couples to consume. From a Christian point of view, marriage is a relationship based on a covenant made in the presence of God. When we were married, we vowed before God that we would live as husband and wife. Our commitment to each other is rooted in our commitment to Jesus Christ. We can't give up on our commitment to each other without breaching our commitment to Christ.

The proverbial picture of a triangle shows the corollary that exists between a couples' closeness to Christ and their closeness with each other. The further they go up the triangle, the closer they get to God and to each other. (Figure A)

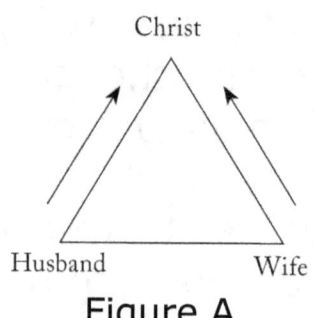

Figure A

It's impossible to be right with God yet bitter toward your spouse. It's a deception when both husband and wife claim to be close to God while their marital relationship is crumbling.

Relationships crumble due to bitterness and hardness of heart. When your heart is hard, God is displeased. When you're close to God, your heart cannot help but soften. His Spirit will guide you to see your own need for forgiveness and prompt you internally to take responsibility for your actions. God's presence is a light to your sin and a reminder of his forgiveness.

It's impossible to be right with God yet bitter toward your spouse.

The Uniqueness of This Book

Our hope is for this book to inspire Christian couples to live by a biblical model of marriage. There are many Christian books on marriage. What this book contributes is the doubly loaded challenge reflected in its title: Just how married do you, as a spouse, want to be? And just how married do you, as a Christian, want to be to Christ, the church's Groom?

While we've made it very practical and personal, the uniqueness of this book is the theological paradigm it promotes. The paradigm we offer is based on a fresh look at Scripture, especially with regard to the mystery of Christ and the church and the mystery of oneness in marriage.

A paradigm is a way of thinking. Paradigms are stubborn; the longer you've had your paradigm, the harder it is to change, even when you realize that the paradigm you have is wrong. A person can hear about and even embrace a new paradigm, and yet remain stuck in the one they realize isn't working.

It usually takes a breakthrough for people to stop living by their paradigms of the past. Many Christian couples, for example, are eager to learn about conflict resolution, decision-making in marriage, and how the biblical concepts of headship and submission ought to play out in marriage. But they hardly ever think about their oneness.

The apostle Paul, however, explains that marriage finds its meaning in the mystery of Christ's union with the church. Consider Ephesians 5:22-33:

Wives, be subject to your own husbands, as to the Lord. For the husband is the head of the wife, as Christ also is the head of the church, He Himself being the Savior of the body. But as the church is subject to Christ, so also the wives ought to be to their husbands in everything.

Husbands, love your wives, just as Christ also loved the church and gave Himself up for her, so that He might sanctify her, having cleansed her by the washing of water with the word, that He might present to Himself the church in all her glory, having no spot or wrinkle or any such thing; but that she would be holy and blameless. So husbands ought also to love their own wives as their own bodies. He who loves his own wife loves himself; for no one ever hated his own flesh, but nourishes it and cherishes it, just as Christ also does the church, because we are members of His body.

For this reason a man shall leave his father and mother and

shall be joined to his wife, and the two shall become one flesh. This mystery is great; but I am speaking with reference to Christ and the church. Nevertheless, each individual among you also is to love his own wife even as himself, and the wife must see to it that she respects her husband.

Due to the gender confusion ravaging the culture, many seem to perceive that Ephesians 5:22-33 is a teaching about manhood and womanhood. But it's a teaching about the mystery of marriage. Ephesians 5:22-33 talks about how the husband should *relate* to his wife and how the wife should *relate* to her husband. The focus of the passage is on becoming one flesh. Oneness has to do with interrelationships.

If the concept sounds abstract, that's because it is. But it generates a ton of applications. Oneness calls for conflict resolution, realistic expectations, truthfulness, vulnerability, excellent listening skills, humble cooperation and an ongoing willingness to forgive.

Too many couples are overly focused on how Christian men and women are to function in their roles individually. There's a treadmill of Christian men trying harder to determine what it means to be a man than what it means for them to be like Christ. Similarly, many Christian women seem to be more intent on honoring and pleasing their husbands than on honoring and pleasing the Lord.3 It's time for Christian couples to start thinking much more seriously about how they ought to function together.

When I (Jim) was a children's pastor, I saw a lot of wives trying so desperately to defer to their husband's leadership, his "headship," that some thought it was better not to pray together at all than for them, as wives, to lead their family in prayer. One of my questions to Christian wives and mothers is, "If neither you nor your husband are discipling your kids in prayer, then who is going to train them in the Lord?"

Ironically, when the *leadership* of the husband becomes a primary focus, the *headship of Christ* is virtually forgotten or ignored. When I (Sarah) ask my seminary students at the beginning of the semester, "What does the Bible mean when it says Christ is the 'head' of the church?" they reply in concert that it basically means that he is Lord and Savior. What my students do not realize entering seminary is that Christ's headship is distinctive. Christ's headship parallels with the headship of the husband in a marriage. As we later explain, headship has to do with oneness.

Notice Ephesians 5:22-33 says nothing about the husband taking steps toward proving or securing his headship. His headship is assumed as a given. The husband "is" the head of the wife no matter what, as Christ is the "Head" of the church.[4] The challenge for Christian couples is to make it their *priority* to build a "one flesh" marriage with their spouse.

The Writing of This Book

Even before we married, we predicted we might someday share a ministry. Sarah's writing has been a springboard toward that end. Thus it's humbling for me (Jim) to have my name on this book. I want everyone to know that Sarah did the hard work of structuring and refining the book. Essentially this book is a sequel to her first book, *Men and Women in the Church,* but in this volume I get the privilege as her husband to be a part of the project.

Here's what we did: Sarah wrote the entire first draft, generating most of the book. She drew from her research and incorporated paragraphs from sermons I had preached at our church. When we revised the book, I dictated my thoughts in portions, and Sarah wrote them down and pieced my thoughts to hers while yet keeping our narrations separate. After that, for the sake of flow, the publisher adapted the manuscript by fusing our narrations, making them less tied to who said what in the earlier drafts. Then Sarah revised the book once again.

Though I (Sarah) was the one who came up with the idea of having Jim coauthor the book, it was hard for me at first to come to grips with my decision. Though it's practically self-evident that we can minister to couples far better as a team than either of us could ever do alone, it was hard for me to scoot over and make room enough for Jim. I was fearful—but not because I didn't trust my husband. My problem was that I didn't trust the church.

As a woman theologian, I feared that some in the church would see my husband as the only viable author of this book, and that I would get lost behind him—because that's exactly what has happened to other public women in church history. So I confessed that to some friends. As a result, I was healed in the process of writing this book, and our marriage was healed some too. We became more "one" as I set aside my fear. It is now at the front of my mind that it's *my* privilege, not just Jim's, to be included in this project. God is so patient to teach me once again that it's always better to live God's way, and God's way is to walk by faith.

The Structure of This Book

Just How Married Do You Want to Be? comprises ten chapters starting with the story of how we got married. We wish we could recount Jim's conversion story too, but his testimony is so gripping that it deserves a separate telling and format. The few highlights of his story that we share in the next chapter will certainly make it clear why we titled our first chapter "An Unlikely Couple."

We have many illustrations of how we have messed up in our marriage and how we are recovering from our choices. Connected to our story is the theological paradigm—the picture of oneness—found in Ephesians 5:22-33. With a careful eye toward Scripture, we cast a biblical vision of how couples can live as one in the daily grind. Unpacking the loaded concepts of headship, submission, mystery, sacrifice and the husband's call to cleave, we try to offer details on how oneness plays out practically. We also offer insight on what it means to develop healthy friendships with people of the opposite sex while yet honoring the oneness of the marriage.

We then move on to the ever-relevant subject of conflict resolution. For once it is established that the husband, though the head, is not the wife's superior, it becomes more urgent to find out how to handle marital conflict. Next, we address the subject of expectations. The content of this section is perhaps the most transferable to every other type of human relationship.

After that, we contend with the very sensitive subject of hot buttons. Our prayer is that married couples will take responsibility for their unresolved issues of the past. This important discussion will then bring us to suggesting ways to build a Christ-centered marriage. There is quite a big difference between a Christ-centered marriage and a self-centered marriage of any sort. Only when a marriage is Christ-centered can a couple maximize their marital oneness.

We end the book by exhorting married couples to participate in community with other authentic followers of Christ. Indeed, the final chapter hails a make-or-break point because when people find the willingness to submit themselves accountably to each other in the Lord, they can gradually find the strength to make changes that beforehand seemed impossible.

Before going any further, we invite you now to pause and pray, not only for your own marriage but also for other marriages, especially the church's marriage with Christ Jesus.

1

AN UNLIKELY COUPLE

Jim and Sarah Sumner are a couple made in heaven. Only heaven would arrange for two people to be wedded with pasts as dissimilar as ours. In 1994 Sarah was on her way to becoming the first woman to graduate with a Ph.D. in systematic theology from Trinity Evangelical Divinity School. She had nineteen years of ministry experience and held an adjunct teaching post at Wheaton College. Jim, by contrast, was a stripper. "Jammin' James Brandon" they called him. Little did he know it, but in October of that year Jim was on his way to Cook County Correctional Facility to hear the gospel. Sarah and Jim lived one mile away from each other for three full years. It was not until June of 1995 that their paths providentially crossed.

The place was Willow Creek Community Church in South Barrington,

Illinois. The time was Saturday morning at a Frontline meeting, a pep rally for the evangelism department. I (Sarah) was thirty-two years old, standing on a platform being introduced as a newly hired member of paid staff. Jim was a new believer in the crowd. I never caught a glimpse of him, but whenever he saw me, inadvertently he said a prayer to God: *Lord, it may be ten years until I'm ready, but if you have a wife for me, please let it be a woman like her.*

Over that summer Jim earned the reputation of being the most on-fire new Christian at Willow Creek. Jim couldn't absorb the Scriptures fast enough. From the moment of his conversion, his desire to learn the Bible dominated all his other interests. Three times a week he attended Willow Creek, two times a week he attended Bible studies, and once a week he was mentored by a neighboring senior pastor.

When finally we met, Jim was starstruck and nervous, almost bumbling in a Clark Kent way. I couldn't help but notice that he was far more handsome than he acted. He seemed flustered and giddy every time we talked. I never would've guessed that he had a sordid past. To me, he seemed impressionable and innocent.

I (Jim) was walking this new journey of being a Christ follower. I was swimming in strange waters. I didn't know the Bible. I didn't know how to speak the Christian language. So how was I going to talk to this woman who had been swimming in these waters all her life?

My discomfort often detoured my thoughts. I remember resorting to my former way of making myself feel secure. *If we were in a bar, I thought, I'd know exactly what to do. I'd capture her attention with eye contact, nod my head and smile. Then I'd take a sip of my drink and slowly start to walk toward her. I'd set down my drink, extend my hand and ask her if she would like to dance.* But in this environment, the reality of my heart was clearly visible. I felt inadequate because Sarah was so scholarly. I had seen her before, carrying lots of books. It intimidated me to talk to her, but regardless I still wanted to be around her. I wanted to be a sponge—to learn all I could from this woman who'd known the Lord for so long.

Soon I found out about a men's group Sarah was teaching at Willow Creek. In essence it was a class for unbelieving men who were interested to wrestle with hard questions. Sarah thought my influence would be good for the other men. I, however, had already made plans to attend a "Contagious Christianity" class that was offered at the same time. When I asked her, "Which class do you think I should take?" she proceeded to explain that while the Contagious Christianity class would be offered again, her class was a one-time thing. So I decided that her class would be the best option.

The class turned out to be great. Discussions were open, even heated sometimes. The men were honest about their doubts and personal struggles. It was the least pretentious group that I (Sarah) have ever taught. Still I have to say that Jim stood out among the others. He was studious and attentive, and he always felt compelled to reach out to the tough guys who were hurting. I specifically remember Jim showing me a letter he had taken the time to write to a rascally fellow classmate named Frank.

Frank was seventy-two years old, widowed and retired, and grieved by his wayward son. Frank was gruff on the outside, yet sensitive and tender on the inside. Sometimes in class, Frank would get riled up, make a melodramatic scene, and storm outside the door to have a cigarette. He consoled himself with cigarettes as a matter of daily habit. Frank *needed* the consolation because he lived in a mental state of anguish. Day by day he tormented himself by hardening his heart and refusing to confess there is a God. But then his guard would drop, and he would plummet into despair because to him, confessing God's existence meant confessing that his son was going to hell. That was Frank's dilemma—choosing one type of agony over the other. If he went the way of God, he would lose his son. If he went the way of atheism, he would lose his soul. Before giving the letter to Frank, Jim asked me to review it.

Jim's letter to Frank had been drafted on the backside of a copy of Jim's resume. I learned two things that changed my perception of him: (1) Jim was actually older than I was—by six years. (2) He had a bachelor's degree in business. Though I was too naive to raise questions about Jim's years in "entertainment," it delighted me to learn that Jim, who had no job, had a background of being gainfully employed. It's funny because it wasn't until eleven years later—until the writing of this book—that I found out that Jim purposely wrote that letter on the back of his resume so I would see it.

At any rate, soon after that Jim and I began to do ministry together with other people. No one had more zeal when proclaiming the truth of Scripture than Jim. His bumbling Clark Kent ways would vanish when he talked about God. Jim was so given over to his newly found faith that some found it difficult to take him seriously. One of my Jewish friends, for instance, openly concluded that Jim was "a flash in the pan"—which is telling because he did so on the night that I consciously concluded just the opposite.

It was November, and we were a party of eight. There was Jim, a Christian woman he hung around with, two Christian wives and their non-Christian husbands, and me and a guy I was dating. The purpose of the party was to talk about the gospel for the sake of the two non-Christian men. After dinner we gathered in a circle in the living room.

I can still see Jim, pouring out his heart, trying to wake up the non-Christians. He was flushed in the face; spit was flying from his mouth; he was fully given over to bearing witness to the things that Jesus Christ had conquered in his life. In agreement with the Jewish guy, my date believed that Jim was just too radical. How could any normal person be sold out to that degree unless they were a "flash in the pan?" I said nothing to my date, but I was silently impressed by Jim's passion. *He loves the Lord the way I do.* That's what I told myself.

Jim was unrefined and unpolished, but he was as personable and earthy as they come. He didn't care what people thought of him. He cared about the truth. He cared about the freedom he had entered. He was New York model-handsome, but so utterly unassuming that people didn't notice what he looked like. All they saw was zeal. I could understand why some people in the group felt overwhelmed by him. But to me, Jim's lack of sophistication and humble artless ways sparkled with a radiant shimmering beauty. Little did I know in the living room that night that Jim was my diamond in the rough.

It's hard to explain the dynamics of that party because both of us had eyes that were veiled. We truly had no idea that we would ever date, much less marry. Every so often in the months of our growing friendship, Jim would plainly tell me that he loved me, but never was it suggestive, and never did it put pressure on our relationship. The first time it happened we were sitting in the atrium among hundreds of other people at Willow Creek. With all the calmness in the world Jim looked at me and said, "Sarah, I look at you across the table, and I love you." Though with anybody else, I would have felt obligated to respond somehow, at least to be polite, with Jim it was okay for me to rest. It never seemed to matter that when he verbalized his love, I never said anything back.

That winter brought an end to the teacher-student aspect of Jim's and my blossoming relationship. No longer could he come to my class. His schedule had changed because he had taken a job as a landscaper. Needless to say, working outside by the sweat of his brow was quite a hard adjustment for him. He went from making $70-$100 an hour to $10 an hour. Instead of dancing as a star, he was working as a digger in the sun. Not only was he forced to transition from the leisure of unemployment, but he also had to retrain his body clock. Jim's new workdays started bright and early at 6:00a.m. All signs from heaven seemed to indicate unequivocally that God had an agenda to transform him by moving him offstage and placing him in obscurity far, far away from the throngs of pretty women who used to stand in line to get his autograph. The stripper in Jim was being stripped. For the next year and a half, Jim worked full time in quasi-anonymity with dirt smeared on his face and a shovel in his hand.

Three more months elapsed. Though we kept in touch, we really weren't together that much. Usually we met serendipitously. We had done some prison ministry and had a few long talks in the Willow Creek parking lot. But our friendship had evolved so naturally that we can't even remember when Jim first told me about his background. All we can recall is one conversation in which I (Jim) was expressing my worry that any woman I wanted to marry would not, in turn, want to marry me. Sarah told me, "Oh Jim, any woman who understands God's grace in her own life will be able to see his grace in yours too."

Willow Creek has this huge atrium filled with tables where people sit and fellowship with one another. One night when we were there, I had on a leather jacket patterned with national flags. It definitely drew attention. I remember seeing Sarah across the room seated at a table with a man who worked on staff. As soon as I approached the table, the man looked up at me, as if staking out his territory, and said sarcastically, "Nice jacket!"

I was nervous and uncomfortable. Up to that moment, I had never intentionally sought out Sarah, even to say hello. At that time, I still wasn't ready, even to tell myself that I felt drawn to her. I can see why she was surprised by my initiative, especially since she had assumed that a relationship was developing between me and the woman friend I hung around with.

For nine months—from August 1995 until late April 1996—we were strictly church friends. Not once did we go out, except to do ministry, and that was almost always with a group. Imperceptibly, however, the kaleidoscope had changed just before the month of May. I (Sarah) remember Jim phoning to say he'd pick me up at 4:00p.m.

"Okay, that sounds great. I'm excited to see you," I said.

"Sarah," he interjected, "you're acting as if we're going on a date. We're just friends."

Feeling a bit rejected, I said defensively, "I know that. But it's my personality to get excited. I could be excited to see my grandmother."

"I want to keep it clear that I'm not trying to be anything but friends," Jim responded. "Now that I'm a Christian, I don't want to lead anyone on or hurt anybody's feelings."

Jim thought he was doing the right thing, being careful not to send mixed signals. Knowing he had already sent mixed signals, I replied too abruptly, "That's fine." Then I added a final remark that belied my futile efforts to pretend as though my feelings were not hurt. "I'll see you today at 4:00, and I'm not excited." Before Jim could respond again, I hung up.

That day we watched two movies back-to-back: *On Golden Pond* and *Dead Man Walking*. There in the theater we sat, maintaining our usual boundaries. We didn't share popcorn, or nudge one another, or even put our elbows on the arm rest. By that time in our friendship, we had only touched four times: twice we had hugged in public, once Jim accidentally touched my leg with the edge of his finger while negotiating his way out of a crowded car on a visit to the juvenile prison, and once we had held hands during a prayer. Later we found out that both us remembered each point of physical contact in keen detail.

Fortunately we had fun that day at the movies. But Jim was a bit distracted because of his anxiety about what he had scheduled for the next day—his dad was coming to town, and Jim had invited me to sit with them at church. Ever since Jim's conversion, he had wanted nothing more than for his dad to meet the Lord.

My habit every morning in that season of my life was to logroll out of bed and pray for an hour on my knees. But on that particular Sunday, I woke up in a funk. I couldn't seem to harness my thoughts. My mind felt like a film reeling backwards. I was too agitated to want to go to church.

What is my problem? I said to myself. I couldn't figure it out. All I could do was wordlessly pray that God would somehow right whatever was wrong.

Forcing myself to rise from the refuge of being nestled on my knees, I somehow made my way into the bathroom and turned on the hot water faucet. As I waited for the water to heat up, all my buried emotions hit the surface. A flood issued forth from my face. I couldn't stop crying, even in the bathtub and even while blow-drying my hair. My eyes would not cooperate with my will. Even when I tried to put on my make up, my eyes kept leaking tears that were blackening my cheeks with wet mascara.

I knew exactly what was wrong. Jim had stolen my heart. I was in love—and totally embarrassed that the feeling wasn't mutual. Desperately I wished I hadn't met him. I wished I didn't even know that he existed. It stung to bear the thought that Jim was in the cosmos destined to be something other than my long-awaited husband.

Meanwhile Jim was looking at his watch, hoping I would get to church on time.

I pulled myself together, put on my best dress and drove to church. When I arrived, there was Jim near the door, beaming with a smile of anticipation and relief. He was standing with his friend, the same woman who had gone with him to the party. She greeted me with the words: "Sarah, you look beautiful."

Comforted by the assurance that at least Jim's friend thought I was pretty, I braced myself for the few remaining hours of my tragic fallen friendship with Jim.

My (Jim's) attention to Sarah's entrance was unprecedented. All of a sudden I saw her as if for the very first time. I stood speechless at her beauty. For a moment I forgot my main objective of wanting her to talk to my dad. But the music was playing, so we said goodbye to my friend and found our seats.

The seating arrangement was Sarah, then me, then my dad, then his wife Bev. Sarah situated herself at a slight angle away from me, and then she started reading her Bible. Though I was completely oblivious, Sarah tells me now that her entire focus was directed to one thing: not crying. She remembers blinking back her tears. Blissful in my ignorance, I leaned in toward her, almost hovering affectionately, as if nothing had been said the day before.

Then bringing myself still closer, I said in a playful tone, "What are you doin'?"

She blinked a few times. "Reading my Bible," she said. "Which part are you reading?"

My questions cheered her up because they were accidentally flirtatious. It couldn't have been more obvious what she was reading; her Bible is oversized with giant print. My fear of commitment could no longer prevail. My heart unleashed my true feelings right in the middle of church. I was treating Sarah as a girlfriend.

After church the four of us went to a good Italian restaurant that I knew was Sarah's favorite. There Bev and I mostly listened as Sarah and my dad engaged in conversation, establishing the basis of the wonderful relationship they continue to enjoy to this day. During that lunchtime, I quietly experienced what it feels like to be in love. I kept gazing at Sarah, marveling at the ease with which she ministered to my dad. I don't remember much about what was said, but I will never forget that day.

After lunch my dad drove the four of us back to the parking lot at church. Before leaving, he wanted to take a picture of us. Sarah thought it was funny that my dad didn't know that we were officially "just friends." It must have been unapparent, especially when I sidled up to her and wrapped my arm securely around her neck. Who could have guessed that I had never been so demonstrative before? We said goodbye, and I followed Sarah home in my car.

As unconvincing as it may sound, I (Sarah) had every intention of ending Jim's and my relationship as soon as we got back to my house. I had planned what I wanted to say: *Jim, it's over. Our friendship has run its course. I know you didn't want this to happen, but it did. I have fallen in love with you, and there's no turning back for me now. I'm sorry, and I'm embarrassed, but we can't ever get together again—because I can't handle it. If anyone asks what happened, feel free to let them know. I fell for you, and you didn't fall for me.*

What happened instead was that Jim followed me into the kitchen where I was getting a glass of water. As usual, I forgot that my landlord kept the drinking glasses on the opposite side of the room away from the sink—just behind where Jim had planted himself. I turned around, retraced my steps, but never quite made it to the cabinet.

To my complete and utter surprise, Jim intercepted me. He clutched me with his arms and held me with an earnestness that washed all my sadness away. We were locked in an embrace that lasted two full hours. But about a minute into it, Jim morphed back into Clark Kent.

"Oh my goodness, what am I doing?" He was breathing as if in a panic.

"Just don't stop," I said.

A few hours later when we experienced our first kiss, the floodgates opened once again. I became a sobbing wet mess.

It was quite a memorable moment for me (Jim). I hadn't kissed in months—not anyone since my conversion. But, hey, I didn't think I'd be that bad. Apprehensively I asked, "What's wrong?"

There was no way for me (Sarah) to divulge the whole truth. Jim could barely admit that we were now more than friends. It would have been way too much for him to hear that I was crying because I knew he was my husband. Besides, it didn't matter. Jim loved me, and I knew it. And I knew that I'd say "yes," to his proposal.

About a week later, the kaleidoscope changed again when Jim said matter-of-factly, "Sarah, we gotta get married."

Without the slightest hesitation, I responded, "Jim, I'll marry you in two days, two weeks, two months, or two years. I don't want you to feel rushed or delayed. Just let me know when, and I'll plan the wedding."

Seven months later we were married on a Sunday morning at Trinity where I got my Ph.D. As we were finalizing plans, I kept telling Jim, "The next time this group of people gets together, one of us will be dead. We only have two chances to be with them all at once—either now at our wedding or later at our funeral. So we better make the most of the opportunity."

We made our wedding weekend as winsome and evangelistic as we could. We took our wedding party and out-of-town relatives to the Saturday night church service at Willow Creek. There were seventy-two people from thirteen different states in our group. After the service, we walked downstairs, enjoyed a catered meal, and then Jim and I did something unconventional: We preached. My part was inspirational; Jim's part was downright disturbing. He spoke with the intent of hoping people would feel convicted of their sin.

Jim was nervous, even nauseous, but his friend Jim Richter followed him into the bathroom and prayed for him out loud, emboldening him to follow through with the plan. What Jim was about to say were things that he had never told his dad, much less my family, most of whom were meeting him for the first time.

Jim started out by saying, "How many of you who know me would say that I'm a man of integrity?" All responded favorably.

When Jim asked similar questions, again the group affirmed his character. But then Jim flipped the conversation on its belly. Indicting himself, he said before the group, "Isn't that something? It's being said that I'm a man of integrity. Yet I've slept with married women, dealt illegal drugs, stolen equipment at my job and functioned as a bookie on the side."

You could have heard a pin drop in that room. One of Jim's friends was sitting there not with his wife but rather with his mistress whose name, of course, didn't match the name plate on the table.

Though it violates the canons of polite company and good taste for a bridegroom to confess the kinds of sins that Jim laid out, we chose to have him to do so because it provided us a way to introduce ourselves as a couple who believes in God's forgiveness. What Jim and I said at our wedding rehearsal dinner is what we're saying again publicly now: Thanks to Jesus Christ, husbands and wives can learn to be one—and that means being partners in forgiveness.

At least for one couple, Jim's message made a palatable difference. They decided that night that they wanted to be more married than they had been. The wife had been harboring such bitterness against her husband that her finger had become too swollen to fit her wedding ring. The husband, for his part, had been detached and self-absorbed. But on the night of our wedding rehearsal dinner, both of them softened their hearts. They apologized to each other and took ownership of the things they had done wrong. After they went home, they talked into the wee hours of the night. They couldn't wait to tell us that as of that night, the wife became able, for the first time in years, to fit her wedding ring on her finger. She wore it to our wedding the next morning.

Our wedding ceremony was joyful. I will never forget walking down the aisle. It felt like being in heaven because everywhere I looked, I saw another person that I loved. Yet as I soon as I joined Jim, everyone else disappeared. He and I existed in a time warp of our own. As we stood before God, we vowed to be married. We vowed to live in oneness as husband and wife. What that means will be discussed in the following chapters.

2

TWO POPULAR MODELS OF MARRIAGE

According to the Bible, marriage is a mystery. Since marriage is a mystery, it cannot be understood unless it is respected as a mystery.

The New Testament Greek word *mystērion* differs from the English word *mystery* in that it points not to a truth that is hidden but rather to a truth that is revealed.[1] A *mystērion* is absurd to those who don't believe in God because a *mysterion* is a supralogical fact—something that cannot be explained merely by the power of human reason. It can only be accepted by the mind that believes in what God has divinely revealed.

In Ephesians 5:31-32, the apostle Paul quotes from Genesis 2:24: "For this reason a man shall leave his father and his mother, and be joined to his wife; and they shall become one flesh." Then he goes on to explain that "this mystery *[mystērion]* is great *[mega]*; but I am speaking with reference to Christ and the church."

The mystery of marriage is the mystery of one flesh that reflects Christ's marriage with the church. Christians accept this as biblical truth, yet often without regarding it as a mystery. Most Christians are taught that marriage is not mysterious at all. Most have learned to see it as a pretty straightforward arrangement: The husband is the head of the house just as Christ is the head of the church. The husband is the leader who makes the final decisions, and the wife—though invited to offer her best input in decision making—is ultimately required to submit.

When I (Jim) first became a Christian, that's what I was taught. So that became my paradigm. Though I went to Bible study and church six times a week and studied the Bible daily for additional hours alone, I never saw anything that contradicted my paradigm—because that was my belief.

But you know what I found out? My paradigm prevented me from seeing the vivid truth that is written down plainly in the Bible. Ephesians 5:23 says the husband is the head of the "wife." In my former paradigm, "head of the wife" was simply a way of saying "head of the house." But there's a notable difference between the words *wife* and *house*.

In Genesis 2, God created Adam and the animals, and then Adam named the animals. Then God said, "It is not good for the man to be alone" (Genesis 2:18). So God put Adam to sleep, pulled a hammer from his side, and built a house for him! And Adam and his house became one flesh.

See how the story no longer fits when we replace the word *wife* with the word *house?* If we replace the word *wife* in Ephesians 5:23 ("the head of the wife") with the word *house* ("head of the house"), not only do we violate the authority of Scripture by changing what it says, but we also change the biblical picture. The husband is one flesh with his wife. He is not one flesh with his house. The husband is no more the head of his house than Christ is the head of a church building.

If the husband is the head "of the wife," and the two of them become "one flesh," is it fair to say the wife is the *body of the husband?* And, by analogy, can we say that the church is the "body" of Christ?

The last time I (Sarah) asked a crowd of seminary students these very questions, some of them were shaking their heads "no." It threw them off to consider the parallel between Christ's headship and the husband's. Because of their paradigm (that the husband is the head of the house), they were slow to recall the well-known biblical fact that Christ's headship has to do with his relationship with the church, his body. Colossians 1:18 says it plainly, "He [Christ] is also head of the body, the church."

Though it might sound incredible at first, the truth of the matter is that Ephesians 5:22-33 presents a picture of oneness—a picture of a head and body. The husband is the head of the wife as Christ is the head of the church. The wife is the body of the husband as the church is the body of Christ. (Figure 2.1)

The husband is the head.

The wife is the body.

Christ is the head.

The church is the body.

Figure 2.1

To put it more starkly, Ephesians 5 conveys a bizarre picture of a male-headed female body. When Jim and I speak together, we like to give the congregation a visual aid: Jim stands behind me, I bow my head, and Jim puts his head above my neck. That way everyone gets a glimpse of the biblical picture. Sounds crazy, but that's why it is labeled a "great mystery."

The language of "head" and "body" and the mystery of "one flesh" is metaphorical. A metaphor, of course, is a literary device that communicates one thing as another; it pretends that *this* is *that*. Eugene Peterson, the highly respected writer of *The Message* translation of the Bible, puts it this way:

> The use of metaphor is not a precise use of language; in fact, it is quite the opposite. A metaphor, instead of pinning down meaning,

lets it loose. The metaphor does not so much define or label as it does expand.... Unfortunately, some exegetes have tried to nail down Scripture's earthy metaphors by exchanging them for abstract truths. But a metaphor is not a truth; it is, taken literally, a lie—an intentional lie.[2]

It's a "lie," so to speak, that two people become one body when they get married. The point is self-evident, really. Jim and I are married. We *are* one flesh, but we don't appear to be one flesh. We don't appear as one flesh because we're not *literally* one flesh; we're *metaphorically* one flesh. There are two important things to remember about metaphors:

1. Metaphors aren't meant to be taken literally.
2. Metaphors aren't meant to be defined.

Since most Christians have never been taught to read metaphors in the Bible *as metaphors,* most believers make the mistake of either taking the metaphors literally or converting them into abstract definitions.

The Biblical Word Head

The word "head," for instance, appears in New Testament Greek as *kephalē*. Technically—if we look at usages *outside* the New Testament—the word *kephalē* can mean either "authority" or "source."[3] But *within* the New Testament, the word *kephalē* consistently refers to a physical head. That's why almost every English Bible that has ever been published in four hundred years translates the Greek word *kephalē* into the English word "head."[4] Biblical examples are numerous. Here's a sample:

- "The very hairs of your *kephalē* are all numbered." (Matthew 10:30; Luke 12:7)
- "When you fast, anoint your *kephalē*, and wash your face." (Matthew 6:17)
- John the Baptist's *kephalē* was brought on a platter. (Matthew 14:11)
- Jesus said of himself that the Son of Man has no place to rest his *kephalē*. (Matthew 8:20; Luke 9:58)

- On the cross, Jesus bowed his *kephalē* and gave up his Spirit. (John 19:30)
- On Jesus' *kephalē* in heaven there will be many crowns. (Revelation 19:12)

Some Christians, being uneasy with metaphors, are quick to define the word *head* instead of reading it as a metaphor. Mistakenly, therefore, it is typically assumed that in Ephesians 5:23, the word *head* really doesn't mean "head" but rather means "authority" or "source." Even among conservatives who think highly of the Bible, there are very few who quote the Bible directly. Rare is the pastor who tells the congregation that the husband is head "of the wife" (Ephesians 5:23)—not the house.

When the Bible isn't quoted, the biblical picture of head-and-body oneness usually gets converted into picture-less definitions or distorted nonsensical images. Consequently, the biblical picture gets lost. There *is* no biblical picture of head and body oneness when the husband is assumed to be the authority or the source of his wife. Though some might argue that they see a different picture—perhaps of a husband being his wife's leader, or perhaps of Adam's rib being used as the source of Eve—they miss the *biblical* picture described in Ephesians [5]. The biblical picture is simple—it's an image of a head and body.

Some, however, want to change the biblical metaphor by simultaneously defining it as "leader" while yet exchanging the word *head* for *brain*. Thus they like to say that the husband is the "brain," and the wife is the "heart." But the Bible does not say that. In fact, it violates the rules of reading comprehension to interpret the biblical metaphors by picturing the *components* of the picture rather than the picture itself. Besides, it doesn't make sense to say a "brain" and a "heart" become "one flesh." A picture of brain attached to a heart isn't a picture of oneness.

There are other problems too with reading Ephesians 5 as if it said the husband is the "brain" and the wife the "heart." In New Testament times the heart, not the brain, was seen as the seat of intellect. Yet another big problem arises when the Bible is misinterpreted in this way because it confirms the false idea that Christ dwells *literally* in the heart, not the brain. Since women are often seen as being more wired for Christianity than men are, the last thing couples need is to be fed a credible lie that say that wives are more spiritual than husbands because they have the "heart" where Christ dwells.[5]

Christians have to be careful not to buy into the paradigms of the world. It's the *world* that says that men, being masculine, are rational and women, being feminine, are emotional. The Bible doesn't say that at all. It flies in the face of Scripture to say that men are not emotional—because that would make them incapable of rejoicing in the Lord or mimicking Christ's anger or grieving about sin with the Holy Spirit. It likewise flies in the face of Scripture to say that women are not rational—because that would make them incapable of following the commandments to renew their minds and meditate on Scripture and take every thought captive to Christ.

According to the Bible, men and women alike are created in the image of God (Genesis 1:26-27); thus both are emotional and rational.

All of these mistakes can be avoided *once* (yes, *once*) we accept the biblical picture as a metaphor. Metaphorically speaking, the husband is the head, and the wife is the body who mysteriously become one flesh.

Consider how dramatically it misses the point if we try to take a different metaphor literally. Jesus said, "I am the door" (John 10:9). Of course, no one ever asks, "What kind of door is Jesus? A screen door? A wooden door? A sliding glass door? What kind of handle does he have?" because that would be to take the metaphor literally. The point of John 10:9 is that Jesus is the door—not the window or the wall. A door, unlike a window, is something that your whole self walks through. Jesus is also not merely *a* door but *the* door—the only entranceway to God.

For many Christian couples, it's a paradigm change to read the word *head* as a metaphor. But the metaphor itself has authority because the metaphor is inspired by God. All Scripture is to be taken seriously, even little words like *a* and *the,* and even metaphors like *head* and *door.* Because all Scripture is inspired by God, it's important to handle Scripture accurately, and part of doing that is to read the biblical metaphors as metaphors.

There are two models of marriage popular in the church—a democratic model and a business model. Both of these models draw from portions of Scripture, yet both are problematic biblically in that both make the mistake of defining the word *head* instead of honoring its authority as a metaphor. Both fail to illustrate the oneness of marriage that God intends for husbands and wives. Neither of these models reflects the mystery of Christ and his union with the church—because neither of these models is mysterious. Thus both are reflective of paradigms that need to be changed.

A Democratic Model of Marriage

In what we might call a *democratic* model of marriage, the husband and wife are seen as equals. A democratic model of marriage rejects the idea of male leadership in the marriage on the basis of the equality of the spouses. Instead of the wife being the only one required to submit, both she and the husband are equally required to mutually submit on the basis of the commandment in Ephesians 5:21 to "be subject to one another in the fear of Christ."

A democratic view of marriage makes sense in light of the original Greek found in Ephesians 5. Verse 22 literally says, "Wives, to your own husbands, as to the Lord." Wives, do *what* to your own husbands? The Greek forces the reader to refer back to the verbal phrase found in verse 21: "be subject to." A democratic view of marriage thus contends that mutual submission overrides the idea of the unilateral submission of the wife.

A democratic reading of Ephesians 5 sees the two main characteristics that should characterize a marriage as (1) mutual submission between husband and wife, and (2) love and respect—the husband loves his wife, and the wife respects her husband. A democratic model can be charted like figure 2.2. Proponents of this model interpret *head* in Ephesians 5:23 as the husband being the "source" of the wife. This view, too, is understandable: Genesis 2:21-22 does, indeed, say that when the first female was created, the Lord God took one of Adam's ribs and fashioned it into the first woman. Since Adam truly was the source of Eve, the headship of the husband in Ephesians 5:23 is considered to be synonymous with the sourcehood, so to speak, of the husband. But exchanging the word *head* for the word *source* leads to significant problems. (Figure 2.2)

Democratic Model of Marriage

Wife is the husband's equal.
Husband's headship is irrelevant.

A wife is to	A husband is to
Submit to her husband	*Submit* to his wife
Respect her husband	Love his wife

Figure 2.2

The biggest problem arises with regard to another passage in the New Testament: "I want you to understand that Christ is the head of every man, and the man is the head of a woman, and God is the head of Christ" (1 Corinthians 11:3). Though it works to say that "man is the source of woman," it simply isn't true that Christ is the "source" of every man—for the source of Adam was the dust (Genesis 2:7). Nor is it true to say that God (alone) was "the source" of Christ—for the source of Christ was both God the Holy Spirit and also the virgin Mary from whom Christ was born (Galatians 4:4).[6]

Another problem with exchanging the word *head* for *source* is that the headship of the husband practically ends up becoming irrelevant. In a democratic model of marriage, the husband, as head, is required to submit mutually to his wife who is *not* the head. Thus the husband's headship—in practical daily terms—means virtually nothing. This reading of Scripture almost ignores the fact that nowhere does the Bible explicitly say that the husband is to submit to his own wife; yet the Bible does say that the wife is to submit to her own husband (Ephesians 5:22).

A Business Model of Marriage

In what we may call a *business* model of marriage, the marriage operates like a business. The husband is the leader, the higher-ranked spouse, and the wife is his assistant, the lower-ranked spouse whom God designed to be the husband's helper.

A business model of marriage certainly appears to be justified by Scripture. It's sensible to think that the biblical word *head* means "leader" since the English word *head* can mean "leader." It also makes sense to think the wife is lower ranked since God created Eve to be Adam's "helper" (Genesis 2:18). It further makes sense to think Ephesians 5:22-23 sees the husband as the authority insofar as it says "Wives, be subject to your own husbands, as to the Lord. For the husband is the head."

A business model reading of Ephesians 5 thus logically concludes that the two main characteristics meant for marriage are (1) leadership and submission—the husband leads and the wife submits, and (2) love and respect—the husband loves his wife, and the wife respects her husband. A business model of marriage can be charted like figure 2.3.

Business Model of Marriage

Husband is the head of the *house*.
Wife is the husband's subordinate.

A wife is to	**A husband is to**
Submit to her husband	*Lead* his wife
Respect her husband	Love his wife

Figure 2.3

A close look at the original Greek and Hebrew, however, reveals the startling truth that a business model of marriage isn't strictly biblical after all. Nowhere in the Scriptures is the husband ever told to "lead" his wife. This idea is very popular, but it doesn't derive directly from God's Word. The apostle Paul never says it in all his letters. Jesus doesn't say it either. Neither does Peter or John. No one in the New Testament ever says it. In fact, *God* never says it in the Old Testament—though many like to think that it's found somewhere in Genesis 1—3.

If the writer of Ephesians had wanted to say the husband is the "leader" of the wife or the "supervisor" of the wife, he could have used other words such as *oikodespotēs,* meaning "master of the house," or *archōn,* meaning "ruler," or *prōtos,* meaning "chief." But instead, the apostle Paul chose *kephalē,* the common Greek word that refers to a physical head.[7]

A close look at Genesis yields another important insight. In Genesis 2:18, Eve is called a "suitable helper" *(ezer kenegdo).* In Hebrew, *kenegdo* means "exact correspondent." So when God created Eve, Adam's *ezer kenegdo,* God gave him a counterpart—a human counterpart—in female form. To unpack the Hebrew more, Adam was given an *ezer.* Though the word *ezer* can be translated into the English word *helper,* it's important to know that an ezer is not necessarily lower-ranked. Since the English word *helper* typically does refer to a lower-ranked assistant, many non-Hebrew speakers assume that *helper* in the Bible means the wife is the husband's subordinate. But in Hebrew the word ezer conveys a powerful type of helper. In fact, sixteen of the nineteen times that ezer appears in the Old Testament, it refers to none other than God.[8] No one can have higher status than God. Two other times ezer refers to military help in time of war. The only other occurrence of ezer in the Bible is in Genesis 2:18—in reference to Eve.

Eve was created as Adam's *ezer*. God designed her specially to live and work and serve as Adam's partner. Adam and Eve were counterparts, male and female created in the image of God (Genesis 1:16-27). Logically it makes sense that God would give the male a female partner—because otherwise he would have been unable to fulfill the divine commandments to "be fruitful and multiply, and fill the earth, and subdue it; and rule" (Genesis 1:28). It was physically impossible for Adam to multiply without Eve. That's why the commandment was issued to them both. God blessed "them" and said to "them" to multiply and fill the earth and subdue it and rule. Here again it's very interesting—and for some another call to a paradigm change—to realize God did not tell Adam to rule Eve. The commandment was for them *both* to be rulers.

Proponents of a business model notoriously make the mistake of presuming that Adam's mistake lay in failing to take leadership of his wife. Those who insist on the husband being the leader are usually the same ones who likewise think that Eve sinned in the Garden by "leading" Adam. The Bible says Eve sinned by eating the fruit (Genesis 3:13). Eve didn't sin by leading her husband. Eve *didn't* lead her husband. It hardly qualifies as an act of leadership for a wife to hand her husband a piece of fruit. Eve "gave" to her husband who was "with her" (Genesis 3:6). Adam is the one who chose to eat. Adam sinned by eating, and Eve sinned by eating. Both violated

God's commandment to "not eat" of the forbidden fruit (Genesis 2:17).

The leadership failure in the Garden of Eden was that Adam and Eve alike both sinned by failing to rule the serpent. Both had the God-given assignment and the God-given authority to rule "over the fish of the sea and over the birds of the sky and over every living thing that moves" (Genesis 1:28)—including the serpent.

So yes, every husband is designed to be a ruler. But he is not designed to rule over his wife. When the husband falls prey to the temptation to rule his wife, he lives out the curse that resulted from original sin. Conversely, when the wife falls prey to the temptation to rule her husband, she lives out the curse too. It's the curse that says the husband will rule over his wife. It's the curse that says the wife will sabotage her husband by desiring to overtake him in subversion. In Genesis 3:16 God said to the woman, "Yet your desire will be for your husband,/and he will rule over you."

Though God ordained the curse as a consequence of sin, God willed for the curse to be reversed. God sent Christ to take the curse away. That is why at Christmas we sing the lines from "Joy to the World":

> No more let sin or sorrows grow
> Nor thorns infest the ground.
> He comes to make
> His blessings known
> Far as the curse is found.

A business model of marriage misinterprets Genesis 3, basing itself wrongly on the curse. More will be said about this later. For now, take note that there are problems with a business model of marriage, and the problems start to mount as soon as *kephalē* is defined as "leader." When Ephesians 5:22-23 says, "Wives, be subject to your own husbands, as to the Lord. For the husband is the head of the wife, as Christ also is the head of the church, He Himself being the Savior of the body," *it no more says* that the husband is the Lord than that the husband is the Savior of the wife.

While followers of a business model of marriage do know that in one sense, they forget it in another. Although they see Christ's lordship as unique, they confuse it with Christ's headship. Thinking that Christ's headship is Christ's lordship, they mistakenly assume that headship is a synonym for leadership. Taking that one step further, they see the *headship* of the husband as the *leadership* of the husband. But headship is distinct, and as we'll see in the next chapter, something huge is lost when we forget that.

3
A DEEPER UNDERSTANDING OF HEADSHIP

In order to make clear how a biblical model of marriage practically functions, it's important to understand the biblical foundations of headship. So before we move ahead to the practical applications found in chapters five through ten, we invite you to join with us in a detailed Bible study that may forever change your marriage and your view of what means to be in the body of Christ.

In what we may call a biblical model of marriage, the language of the Bible is carefully kept intact. Instead of *head* being defined as "source" or "authority," the word *head* is understood as meaning "head." In a biblical model of marriage, the headship of the husband is quintessentially Christian because it's rooted in the mystery of Christ.

Headship Communicates a Picture

Headship is a relational term. Headship has to do with connectedness. It implies oneness with a body. Headship carries the notion of being radically associated with another.

In every case in the New Testament in which *kephalē* (head) is used, the connotation it conveys is physical. The word either refers literally to someone's physical head, or it refers metaphorically to a picture of a head in relation with a body.[1]

When the Bible says the husband is the "head" of the wife, it means the husband is connected to his wife to such an extent that he shares an identity with her. Her flesh is his flesh, and his flesh is hers. Together they form a "one flesh" union. So shared is their identity that it's silly for the two of them to compete. Husband and wife are not meant to be opponents. They are meant to be colaboring partners. What head would ever compete with its own body? What body would ever compete with its own head? Jealous competition between spouses doesn't happen when a couple comprehends the spiritual mystery that marriage is a union of one flesh.

If headship is considered to be a trump card, then a husband might be tempted to use his headship for the sake of his own advantage. Rightly understood, however, headship is a metaphor that describes the husband's closeness with his wife.

Headship has to do with oneness. God's headship of Christ reveals God's oneness with Christ. Christ's headship of the church reveals Christ's oneness with the church. The husband's headship of the wife reveals his oneness with the wife. On the basis of these biblical parallels, it is possible to discern how headship ought to operate in marriage.

God's Headship of Christ

God heads Christ by being one with him. Christ is God in the flesh, God with skin on (John 1:1, 14). Christ is the incarnate body of God. As the apostle Paul explains it, "For in Him

[Christ] all the fullness of Deity dwells in bodily form" (Colossians 2:9). Jesus said it even more plainly, "I and the Father are one" (John 10:30). This oneness is so radical that "all things" God created came into being by Christ, the Word of God, who became flesh (cf. John 1:1-3, 14). Nineteenth-century theologian Charles Hodge put it boldly: "According to the Scriptures, the Father created the world, and the Son created the world."[2]

The oneness of Christ and God reaches still further. For it is Christ who redeems the world, and Christ who will one day judge the world. In Isaiah 43:1, the prophet says:
> But now, thus says the lord, your Creator...
> And He who formed you,...
> "Do not fear, for I have redeemed you;
> I have called you by name; you are Mine!"

The prophecy is stunning insofar as it reveals that God, the Redeemer, is none other than the Creator of the world! God the Redeemer is Christ.

Amazingly, God the Redeemer is also the Judge. As the apostle John explained it, "For not even the Father judges anyone, but He has given all judgment to the Son" (John 5:22). The oneness of God and Christ is so fundamentally shared that it is virtually synonymous to say:
- *God* is a righteous Judge. (Psalm 7:11)
- *The Lord* is our Judge. (Isaiah 33:22)
- There is *only one* Law giver and Judge. (James 4:12)
- [God] has given all judgment to the *Son.* (John 5:22)

In all these shared activities, we see that God heads Christ by exercising oneness with him. God created the world in oneness with the Word who supernaturally became human flesh. God redeemed the world in oneness with Christ who by his crucifixion conquered death. God will judge the world in oneness with Christ to whom all final judgment has been given. God heads Christ in this demonstrative way "so that all will honor the Son even as they honor the Father" (John 5:23).

Christ's Headship of the Church

The same exercise of oneness happens all over again in the way that Christ heads his body, the church (Colossians 1:18). Notice, Christ is the head—but not just plain and simple. Christ is the head *of the church* (Ephesians 5:23). It's enlightening to consider what John 1:1 does *not* say. It does not say, "In the beginning was the head, and the head was with God, and the head was God." Christ was not revealed as "head" until *after* he founded the church. Consider Ephesians 1:

> [God] raised [Christ] from the dead and seated Him at His right hand in the heavenly places, far above all rule and authority and power and dominion, and every name that is named, not only in this age but also in the one to come. And [God] put all things in subjection under [Christ's] feet, and gave [Christ] as head *(kephalē)* over all things to the church, which

is His body, the fullness of Him who fills all in all. (Ephesians 1:20-23)

The language conveys a picture of Christ connected to the church, standing above all things. Here's the catch. Since *Christ* is above all things, *the church* is above all things, being that the church is Christ's body. Since the *head* is above all the things, the head's body is above all things. The metaphorical picture reveals the awe-inspiring news that "under Christ's feet" means "under the church" since Christ's feet are part of Christ's body. (Figure 3.1)

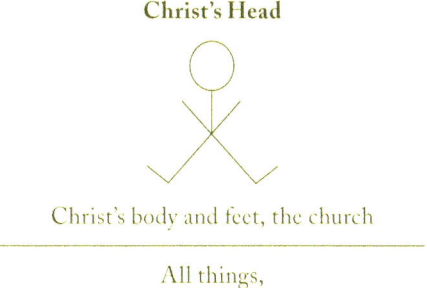

Figure 3.1. Since the head is above all things, the head's body is above all things.

The picture in figure 3.1 offers a glimpse of Christ, the head, reigning with his body, the church. To say this is completely biblical. Three different times the New Testament says that the church will reign with Christ (2 Timothy 2:12; Revelation 5:10; 22:5). Christ reigns *with* his bride, the church, precisely *because* the church is his body. Incidentally, that explains why the church, "the saints," will one day "judge angels" (1 Corinthians 6:2-3).

Christ's Headship of Men

Metaphorically speaking, headship is always masculine. There is no such thing as feminine headship. A wife can no more be the head of her husband than she could ever be male. That's why headship within marriage is for the husband. Headship has nothing to do with the husband's personality or giftedness or his level of maturity or his health—or even his leadership. Regardless of all these things, he is the head of his wife.

The metaphorical concept of headship is physically reflected in the universal fact that the husband is less vulnerable *bodily* than his wife. The apostle Peter (who unquestionably was married; see Luke 4:38) thus admonished Christian husbands:

> You husbands in the same way, live with your wives in an understanding way, as with *someone weaker* [my emphasis], since she is a woman; and show her honor as a fellow heir of the grace of life, so that your prayers will not be hindered. (1 Peter 3:7)

A lot of men think it's biblical for them to be the leaders of the marriage, and one reason why they think this is because they think "weaker vessel" means that their wife is not as capable as they are. Some would even say that women are inferior to men in a leadership capacity. So it's critical to unpack what "weaker vessel" means in Greek.

I (Sarah) will never forget my own process of praying to God about what it means to be a "weaker vessel." One of the first things I did was reach for the dictionary and look up the English word *weak.* Here's what I found:

1. a) Lacking in strength of body or muscle; not physically strong

b) Lacking vitality; feeble; infirm

2. Lacking in skill or strength in combat or competition

3. Lacking in moral strength or will power; yielding easily to temptation, the influence of others, etc.

4. Lacking in mental power or the ability to think, judge, decide, etc.

5. Lacking ruling power, or authority

6. Lacking in force or effectiveness

7. a) Lacking in strength of material or construction; unable to resist strain, pressure, etc.; easily torn, broken, bent, etc.

b) Not sound or secure; unable to stand up to attack...

12. a) Ineffective; unconvincing; b) faulty

Under all these definitions, the dictionary reads, "The broadest application of these words basically implies a *lack* or *inferiority* of physical, mental or moral strength" (my emphases).

As soon as I saw the word *inferior*, I fell to my knees and started praying, "Lord, I've never consciously thought of myself as being inferior to men. But it's right there on the page. I'm a woman, a 'weaker vessel,' and I guess that means I'm 'inferior.' So now what?"

I remembered being taught in seminary not to resort to a dictionary, so I grabbed my Greek Bible, found 1 Peter 3 and checked to see what Greek word Peter used: *asthenēs.*

"Oh Lord," I said in prayer, "Is it the same word as I think it might be?"

Indeed, it was. When I turned to 1 Corinthians 1, the word appeared once again: *asthenēs.* Except this time, it was not referring to a woman. This time it was referring to God. "The weakness *[asthenēs]* of God is stronger than men" (1 Corinthians 1:25).

The *asthenēs* of God? It is heresy to suggest that God could ever be inferior. The Lord God reigns supreme above all. The very idea of God's inferiority is preposterous.

I turned to 2 Corinthians 13:4 and found the same word again. Except in this case, it was describing Jesus. "For indeed He was crucified because of weakness *[asthenēs].*" Surely we can't say that at Calvary our Lord was "inferior" to the devil. Even on the cross, Jesus was superior to the devil. According to the Gospel of John, Jesus was crucified because he himself used his own "initiative" and "authority" to lay down his own life (John 10:18).

Right then, in that memorable moment, I was assured that, since *asthenēs* can't mean "inferior" in 1 Corinthians 1:25 or 2 Corinthians 13:4, it's biblical to believe that *asthenēs* means something else in 1 Peter 3:7.

Technically there's no problem with translating *asthenēs* into English as "weak." The problem arises when a person comes to think the dictionary definition of the English word *weak* directly correlates to Peter's use of the word in Greek. My students have suggested that perhaps *asthenēs* can be translated as "humility" or "compassion." Watch how this plays out, first with *humility:*
- God's *humility* is stronger than humanity.
- Christ was crucified because of *humility.*
- Women are more *humble* than men.
And again, with *compassion:*
- God's *compassion* is stronger than humanity.
- Christ was crucified because of compassion.

- Women are more *compassionate* than men.

Though both words might at first seem promising, as it turns out, neither one fits. To begin with, neither *humility* nor *compassion* fits into the semantic range of the Greek word *asthenēs* which literally means "strengthless." Second, though it may be true that God's humility is stronger than humanity (an odd thing to say) and that Christ was crucified because of his humility, it is not true that women are more humble than men. Likewise, though Christ was crucified, in part, because of his compassion, and though women are often perceived as being more compassionate than men, it isn't necessarily true that women are more compassionate than men. Besides that, it doesn't make sense to say the "compassion of God" is stronger than humanity. But it works if we use the word *vulnerability*.

- The *vulnerability* of God is stronger than men.
- Christ was crucified because of *vulnerability.*

- Women are more physically *vulnerable* than men.

Each verse now makes sense. The weakness of God is not divine inferiority; the weakness of God refers to God's willingness to be relationally vulnerable. God's nature isn't physical, but it's his nature to be relationally involved with people. The Bible is filled with examples of God making himself vulnerable either to be pleased or displeased, delighted or angered or appalled or grieved by his people. Still God relates to people as God, nothing less.

The weakness of Christ refers to Christ's physical crucifixion. In heaven it was impossible to kill the Son of God, but on earth he became vulnerable to death. The weakness of wives, likewise, refers to their physical vulnerability that is comparatively weaker than their husband's.

I (Sarah) work out almost daily, and Jim hardly works out at all, yet I still don't have the muscle mass that he does. Jim has to be reminded sometimes to be gentle with me because he forgets how much weaker

I am. When we took dance lessons, our instructor told us that the number one injury on the dance floor is when the male partner accidentally breaks the female's fingers.

Pregnancy makes women even more vulnerable. Pregnant women aren't able to run as fast or exert themselves with the same force because a pregnant woman's body is devoting itself sacrificially to the child.

Some women are physically stronger than some men. That may be true, but no man's body is vulnerable to a woman's body in the same way that hers is to a man's. A man's body is closed where a woman's body is open. A man can be assaulted, but he cannot be raped by a woman. It's the exception for a woman to be stronger than a man. Men naturally have more muscle mass than women.

Men *are* physically vulnerable, of course. Both men and women can be attacked by bullets and disease. It's just that women are more physically vulnerable than men—within the context of their relationships with men. So Peter's admonition is for husbands not to use the physical advantage that they, as men, have over their wives. If a husband exploits his wife's greater physical vulnerability—which enables her to give birth—then God will hinder his prayers. For when a husband uses his *body* against his wife, he uses his headship against his wife as well.

That's why Christ gives special headship lessons to men. As "head of every man" (1 Corinthians 11:3), Christ shows every man what it's like to be treated in an understanding way. Christ heads men without exploiting men. Jesus could have crushed the men who nailed him to the cross. But he didn't. He didn't take advantage of his power. He didn't summon a legion of angels. He didn't kill anybody on the spot. But he could have.

I (Jim) am inspired by Christ's headship. I want to head Sarah the way Christ heads me. Jesus Christ lifted me out of a pit. He uses his power to free me, so that I can give freely to others. I want to use my influence to help my wife develop and contribute all she can to God's kingdom. Having Christ as my head makes me want to be as loving as Jesus. I want to love Sarah sacrificially as Christ loves me.

The Distinctiveness of Christ's Headship

Most believers, especially Protestants, tend to overlook Christ's headship. Without doing so on purpose, we miss the biblical fact that Christ's headship is distinctive both from his lordship and his saviorhood.

Earlier I (Sarah) mentioned that my seminary students have said their concept of Christ wouldn't change at all if the Bible no longer said Christ is "head." From their perspective, the biblical phrase "Christ is the head of the church" means the exact same thing as "Christ is Lord of the church."

Rarely do we think about Christ's headship. We think about Christ as Lord. We thank him for being our Savior. But rarely do we speak about *being in relationship* with Christ our head. We might glibly say that "Christ is the head of the church," but usually when we do that, we think of it in a way that is so totally abstract, it doesn't move us. Almost never do we say that Christ is the head of *me* and Christ is the head of *us.*

We devalue the word *head* when we reduce the biblical picture of headship to mere words. I am guilty of doing this myself. It was only when I realized that *head* in the New Testament is meant to be read metaphorically that I finally figured out that Jesus is truly my head. It was sort of like hearing a thousand times over that God loves me, and then suddenly being hit with a brand new realization—oh my goodness, God loves me! The more I ponder the truth—that Christ is my head, the more amazed I feel to be in relationship with him.

Once we begin to see ourselves as belonging to Christ our head, we start to understand how much we all matter to God. Once we see that we—together—are members of Christ's body, we finally get a notion of why it's so important for the church to strive for unity in Christ.

Church *disunity* is promoted intellectually by the way so many Christians, particularly in the West, individualize their connection to the Lord. It's as if we all believed that having "a personal relationship with Christ" is completely unrelated to being one of the many members of Christ's body.

It's as if we believe that having "a personal relationship with Christ" is completely unrelated to being one of the many members of Christ's body.

Perhaps even less do married couples in the church consciously think of themselves as being members of each other—as being a head and body union that symbolizes Christ's union with the church. We cannot be "more married" to each other without being more surrendered to Christ. The husband is the wife's head, and the wife is the husband's body. We are still trying to absorb these profound truths. We are "in Christ" because we are Christ's body. That's already settled. Our *relationship with Christ* is what fluctuates. We are responsible to follow Christ each day—to die to ourselves each day—in order to practice oneness in our marriage.

It's helpful to wrestle with questions such as: Would it change my view of marriage if the word "head" *(kephalē)* were removed from Ephesians 5? Would I even miss the word "head" *(kephalē)* at all? Or would I rationalize things and say, "Well, it really doesn't matter if "head" *(kephalē)* is there or not because the thrust of the passage is to say that Christ is Lord, the leader of the church, and that a husband, by analogy, is therefore the leader of his wife"?

Headship does not mean lordship. Husband and wife are to relate as head and body—not as body and lord. The Bible says the husband is the *kephalē* of his wife, not the *kyrios* (Lord) of his wife. When Christians are led to believe that headship and lordship are synonymous, they logically conclude that since Christ is the Lord of the Church, the husband is the lord of his wife.

The Lordship of the Husband?

This mistaken belief becomes yet more entrenched when people go on to misinterpret other verses such as 1 Peter 3:6: "Sarah obeyed Abraham, calling him lord." It is assumed that she did so because Abraham was her leader. But God told Abraham to "listen to" his wife. There is a conceptual correlation in the Old Testament between listening and obeying. For instance, in Deuteronomy 11:26-27, God says, "See, I am setting before you today a blessing and a curse: the blessing, if you listen to the commandments of the Lord your God, which I am commanding you today." The word *listen* here means "obey." So Sarah was told to "obey" Abraham, and Abraham was told "to listen" to her—which essentially means the same thing. When Abraham and Sarah deferred to one another, they were ultimately following God.

Another verse that's often misread is Ephesians 5:22, "Wives, be subject to your own husbands, *as to the Lord*" [my emphasis]. While it's true that wives are commanded to submit, it is not true that husbands are supposed to be followed indiscriminately. The wife is to submit to her husband, but not if it dishonors the Lord. In other words, she is not required to submit to her husband as if *he himself* were the Lord. According to Ephesians 4:5, there is only "one Lord," Jesus Christ.

The wife's submission to her husband is guided by her submission to the Lord. So if the husband tries to persuade his wife to sin, it is better for her not to submit. Countless examples illustrate the point. If the husband is physically abusive, the wife is not to submit. If he tells her to get a breast enlargement, she doesn't have to submit. If he tells her not to hold him accountable because he is held accountable by God, it is better for her not to submit. If he asks her to lie, she should not submit. Think of Ananias and Sapphira in Acts 5. God struck Sapphira dead. Sapphira was not excused from punishment as if she were a excused from punishment as if she were a mere victim of her husband's sinful leadership.

Quite the opposite—she (just as Eve in Genesis 3) was held responsible by God.

The husband is the wife's head—not her lord and not her savior.

I (Jim) can't be responsible for Sarah's thoughts and actions because I don't have control of her will. She has *response-ability*—the ability to respond—because she, as a woman, is created in the image of God. The same principle holds true for husbands. Husbands are responsible for themselves. They are called by God to be Godlike and Christlike in their headship. No husband, however, is told to act as "Lord" or "Savior" of his wife. The husband is the wife's head—not her lord and not her savior.[3]

To the well-intentioned reader who's unacquainted with Greek syntax, it could very well appear that in Ephesians 5:23—"For the husband is the head of the wife, as Christ also is the head of the church, He Himself being the Savior of the body"—Paul equates the husband's headship with Christ's divine power to save. But in fact, Paul did just the opposite. He articulated the *difference* between the husband and Christ. He qualified the analogy, explaining that the analogy breaks down. Preeminent scholar A.T. Robertson says that there is a "comparison" between the husband's headship and Christ's headship "but with a tremendous difference"—that Christ uniquely is Savior—"which Paul hastens to add."[4]

The apostle continues to speak of *Christ alone* in Ephesians 5:26-27:

> So that He might sanctify her, having cleansed her by the washing of water with the word, that He might present to Himself the church in all her glory, having no spot or wrinkle or any such thing; but that she would be holy and blameless.

In first-century Jewish weddings, every bride would be given a cleansing bath, then arrayed in her bridal dress, and then brought to the bridegroom. Paul's point is that *Christ,* the church's groom, does the cleansing and presenting—unlike a traditional Jewish groom, who is uninvolved in the process. As Leon Morris puts it, "Paul is writing about a marriage that is unique, one in which all the preparation is done by Christ."[5]

Christ prepares the church to meet him in glory. Husbands can't do that for their wives because husbands themselves are being prepared by Christ for heaven. No husband has the power to sanctify himself—much less sanctify his wife—as if his headship made him holier than his wife.[6] The husband is not called to be his wife's "spiritual leader." The term "spiritual leader" isn't even found in Scripture. Yes, the husband is commanded to minister to his wife, but she is commanded to minister to him too. Both, as believers, are expected to apply all the teachings in the Bible to their marriage.

In Ephesians 5, the husband specifically is commanded to love his wife as Christ also loved the church. Yet here again, the analogy between husbands and Christ breaks down. The parallel is limited because while Christ is head *and* Lord *and* Savior of the church, the husband is strictly the "head" of the wife. But his headship is significant, as we will point out when we introduce a biblical model of marriage.

4

A BIBLICAL MODEL OF MARRIAGE

A biblical model of marriage is mysterious. It's a head and body union of one flesh. A biblical model of marriage takes into account what the whole Bible says about marriage and what it says about being a member of Christ's body. To be a faithful spouse is to be wedded to Jesus Christ along with being married to a person. In a biblical model of marriage, the couple honors Christ as Lord and Savior. Christ alone is treated as the leader of the marriage because Christ alone is Lord. The husband, by contrast, is the head—not of the marriage but "of the wife" (Ephesians 5:23). The wife, therefore, is the body of the husband. Together they mysteriously are one. Though all of Scripture is relevant to the life of Christ's bride, the church, the clearest blueprint for marriage is found in Ephesians 5:22-33.

The Commandment Is to Love

In Ephesians 5:22-33, the husband is commanded—no less than three times—to "love" his wife. In all three instances, the word *love* occurs grammatically in verbal form. It does not occur as an adverb. The adverb *lovingly* is nowhere to be found in Ephesians 5. Yet it's common for Christian husbands to think it comes straight from Scripture for the husband to "lovingly lead" the wife by serving as her spiritual leader.

This belief is wrong. It is not good exegesis when reading Ephesians 5:25 to change the verb *love* into the adverb *lovingly* and add the word *lead* into the text. The verse says, "Husbands, love your wives just as Christ also loved the church." It does *not* say, "Husbands, lovingly lead your wives just as Christ also lovingly leads the church."

No responsible Christian would ever stand for changing the golden rule in this same way. To say the commandment ranked second in all of

Scripture is to "lovingly lead others as you lovingly lead yourself" would be too great a stretch. It is likewise a stretch to say that *love* in Ephesians 5 means "lovingly lead."

The passage actually loses its literary effect when the word *love* is replaced by "lovingly lead." Ephesians 5 juxtaposes two opposites—love and hate:

> So husbands ought also to *love* their own wives as their own bodies. He who *loves* his own wife *loves* himself; for no one ever *hated* his own flesh, but nourishes and cherishes it, just as Christ also does the church. (Ephesians 5:28-29, my emphases)

The literary effect is lost when the word *hate* is juxtaposed to a phrase ("lovingly lead") that does not correspond as an opposite. Similarly, the correlation of the husband's call to "love" his wife and the wife's call to "respect" her husband becomes less clear when the word *love* is understood as "lovingly lead." When the biblical text is interpreted in this way, couples end up thinking that Paul is telling wives to respect their husband's *leadership*—instead of respecting the husband himself.

A Distorted View of Headship

Someone might argue that the problem in interpreting Ephesians 5 is not about changing the word *love* to "lovingly lead"; the problem, rather, happens when the word *head* is misinterpreted as "ruler" or "chief" instead of as "servant leader."

If by the term *servant leader,* it is meant that the husband serves his wife by exalting her in the way that God exalts Christ to the highest seat of power, and Christ exalts the church to reign with him in oneness over "all things," then *servant leader* could almost be synonymous with *head.* But not quite—because it still, in that case, would fail to communicate the mystery of oneness. Only when head is interpreted as "head" does the metaphorical picture come to mind.

As we have repeatedly said, marriage presents a picture of

oneness—a picture of a head and body. The husband is the head of the wife as Christ is the head of the church. The wife is the body of the husband as the church is the body of Christ. (Figure 4.1)

The husband is the head.

The wife is the body.

Christ is the head.

The church is the body.

Figure 4.1

Before we were married, there were people in our church who tried to talk Sarah out of marrying me (Jim). They envisioned her marrying a president or a senior pastor. They were concerned because of my short time of being a Christian. They were worried about Sarah settling for someone with a limited education. But the main question raised was, "How could Jim be her spiritual leader?"

Not one person ever asked her, "Do you respect Jim enough to submit to him as his wife?" or "Does Jim love you sacrificially as Christ loves the church?" No one pressed the question, "Is Jim committed to Jesus?" They were more concerned about my *ability to lead*

Sarah than my *connection to our head, Jesus Christ.*

The people who were worried didn't see the biblical picture. The picture holds the power to take our breath away. I (Sarah) gasp at the thought, when I really contemplate it, that Christians are nothing less than Christ's body. We are his hands! We are his feet! How can this possibly be? It's a mystery—a miracle—that we can be so joined with Jesus Christ.

This very miracle is reflected in the mystery of marriage. The husband and wife are one. She is his body, and he is her head. Spiritually they are meshed into one flesh.

I (Jim) might have treated Sarah better early in our marriage if I had understood that she is my body—that she is that much of me. I never thought of Sarah being my body. I knew I wasn't her leader, but knowing that didn't help me to grasp the biblical truth that I'm her head.

Ephesians 5:22-33

The whole passage in Ephesians 5 makes much more sense—it practically leaps out from the pages—when it is read from the perspective of a biblical model of marriage. Once we have a paradigm that allows for mystery, the coherency of the text becomes self-evident. So let's walk through the whole passage.

Wives, be subject to your own husbands, as to the Lord (v.22). Just because the wife is told to submit does not mean that the husband is told to lead. If that were so, then on principle Ephesians 5:21, "and be subject to one another" (the phrase that supplies the verb for verse 22) would be a tacit inverse command for everyone to lead each other. The thrust of the command is not for Christians to lead one another. The point is for Christians to assume a humble posture when personally relating with one another. No one is teachable or accepting of correction apart from a posture of submission.

There is no denying in a biblical model of marriage that the wife is commanded to submit to her own husband or that the husband is her head. In fact, the wife is commanded to submit to her own husband *because* he is her head.

For the husband is the head of the wife, as Christ also is the head of the church, He Himself being the Savior of the body. But as the church is subject to Christ, so also the wives ought to be to their husbands in everything (vv.23-24). When you think of the biblical picture, it's obvious why the wife is commanded to be subject to her husband "in everything." How could she not be? As his body, she is attached to him as head in everything. It might sound funny for Scripture to tell wives to be subject to a head they're already attached to, but that's how it goes in Scripture. In Colossians 3:3-5, the apostle Paul writes like that again: "For you have died and your life is hidden with Christ in God.... Therefore consider the members of your earthly body as dead." It's common in Scripture for God to command us to be who we are in Christ.

Husbands, love your wives, just as Christ also loved the church and gave Himself up for her (v.25). Here the biblical directive for husbands is not for them to submit but to sacrifice themselves for their wives. This aspect of Ephesians 5 is often disregarded or overlooked.[1] So many men, as we will talk about later, think sacrificing themselves means saving their wives life if ever her life is jeopardized or in danger. Many Christian husbands simply haven't been taught that it's biblical—and manly—for a husband to understand that he is not entitled to have his own way just because he is the head.

So husbands ought also to love their own wives as their own bodies. He who loves his own wife loves himself; for no one ever hated his own flesh, but nourishes and cherishes it, just as Christ also does the church (vv.28-29). Again, the biblical picture makes this passage vivid. The husband is commanded to love his wife—for in doing so, he loves his own body! When a husband understands that his wife is "his own flesh," he can't help but love her. No husband goes around hating his own flesh—buying presents for himself he doesn't want.

By God's design, the husband is inclined to make choices for himself that accord with his own preferences. So when a husband starts to realize that his wife's preferences are part of his identity as a husband, he begins to understand that in loving her, he is loving himself. When a husband truly cherishes his wife, he will nourish her with positive attention. He will delight to watch her grow because her growth will be of benefit to him. As there's no competition between a body and a head, so there's no competition between a wife and a husband who are grounded in the Lord.

For this reason a man shall leave his father and mother and shall be joined to his wife, and the two shall become one flesh (v.31). The husband is commanded to cleave to his wife—as if she were his own body. It's biblical for a husband to include his wife, not for the purpose of using her to facilitate his own agenda but rather for the sake of being one with her in the likeness of Christ and the church.

This mystery is great; but I am speaking with reference to Christ and the church (v.32). The mystery of the marriage of Christ and the church is so marvelous and mysterious that it can be explained only in metaphorical language that conveys a shocking picture of radical oneness. Unlike any definition, the metaphorical picture awakens us to the unfathomable truth that Christ invites the church to marry him (Revelation 19:7-9). As Christians we are destined to share in all the riches of Christ.

Nevertheless, each individual among you also is to love his own wife even as himself (v.33). There it is again, the mystery that says when a husband loves his wife as himself, he is loving himself—because he and his wife are one. Indeed, this is the mystery of one flesh. Now consider the last part of verse 33: "*and the wife must see* to it that she respects her husband." Again, the biblical picture shows that when a wife respects her husband, she is respecting herself. She must respect herself as she respects him—because she is her husband's body.

If we contrast the command in Ephesians 5:33 ("The wife must see to it that she respect her husband") with the curse in Genesis 3:16 ("Your desire will be for your husband"), we can start to see that it's not God's will for the wife to "desire" (that is, dominate or cling to) her husband. God wants her to "respect" him. In fact, she herself is to "see to it" that she respect her husband no matter what. It is not the husband's job to demand the respect of his wife. She is to respect him regardless.[2]

Conversely, if we contrast the command in Ephesians 5:33 ("Each individual among you also is to love his own wife even as himself") with the curse in Genesis 3:16 ("And he will rule over you"), we can start to see that it's not God's will for the husband to "rule" (that is, dominate or put down) his wife. God wants the husband to "love" her no matter what. (Figure 4.2)

Biblical Model of Marriage

Husband is the head of the *wife*.
Wife is the husband's body.

A wife is to	A husband is to
Submit to her husband	*Sacrifice himself* for his wife
Respect her husband	Love his wife

Figure 4.2

A biblical model of marriage therefore says there are *three* main dynamics (not just two) between husband and wife: (1) oneness between head and body; (2) sacrifice and submission; (3) love and respect.

Comparing the Three Models

Whereas a biblical model of marriage prominently features the great mystery *(mega mystērion)* of marriage (see figure 4.2), the other two models do not. A democratic model of marriage essentially sees both husband and wife as two equal individuals who relate to each other as colleagues. By contrast, a business model of marriage essentially sees the husband and wife relating within the structure of a hierarchy (see figure 4.3).

Three Models of Marriage

Democratic Model	Equal + Equal	= Collegiality (of two colleagues)
Business Model	Leader + Assistant	= Hierarchy (of authority and subordinate)
Biblical Model	Head + Body	= Mystery (of head and body)

Figure 4.3

How tempting it is to convert the biblical metaphors into clear-cut definitions that demystify the mysteries of God! Eugene Peterson says it well: "There is a mind, too common among us, that is impatient with mystery. Mystery, these minds assume, is what pastors and theologians are paid to get rid of."[3]

So now, you decide. Which is more biblical? A husband and wife paired as two equal entities? A husband and wife joined as authority and subordinate? Or a husband and wife united as head and body? The answer is evident, and yet its validity is underscored further when it comes to the subject of divorce.

Why God Hates Divorce

When the Greek word *kephalē* (head) is defined—and thereby displaced by words such as "authority" or "source"—married couples in the church (particularly in contemporary Western culture) tend to minimize the tragedy of divorce. Only when *kephalē* (head) is interpreted to mean in English the same thing it means in Greek can readers of the Bible begin to see in graphic form why God hates divorce (Malachi 2:16).[4]

What the biblical picture shows is a horrible bloody scene. When a head and body union radically disconnect from each other, all of heaven knows there a rupture, a great tearing, of one flesh. Divorce incurs a terrible violation. Professor David Gushee reports that "from the children's perspective, their parents' divorce is almost always the most significant event in their lives." Citing Judith Wallerstone's research, Gushee says further, "While ... at least some of the time adults are able to absorb divorce and even benefit from the experience, this is less often the case for children. Divorce leaves its mark, not just for a brief period of time, but for a lifetime."[5]

William Barclay offers an interesting commentary on Jesus' teaching on divorce in Matthew 19:1-6. Barclay notes that Jesus took things "back to the very beginning, back to the ideal of creation."

> In the case of Adam and Eve divorce was not only inadvisable; it was not only wrong; it was completely impossible, for the very simple reason that there was no one else whom either of them could possibly marry.

Jesus, Barclay observes, saw Adam and Eve as "the pattern and the symbol of all who were to come."[6]

It is not so disturbing to envision a leader departing from his assistant or vice versa. And it is not that big a deal to see two individuals, both equal and independent, choosing to move on their own ways. But it is utterly disconcerting to imagine a physical body being wholly amputated from its head. How might the divorce rate dramatically drop if everyone in the church were to acknowledge the dreadful picture—the decapitation—that happens when a couple breaks up? No wonder Jesus said, "What therefore God has joined together, let no man separate" (Matthew 19:6).[7]

5
PRACTICING ONENESS IN THE GRIND OF DAILY LIVING

So far we have said that a biblical model of marriage involves a head-body, sacrifice-submit, love-respect dynamic. The husband is the head of his wife, and the wife is the body of her husband. The husband sacrifices himself for his wife, and the wife submits to him. The husband loves his wife, and she respects him. When a biblical model of marriage is played out, the relationship between husband and wife provides a picture of Christ's marriage with the church.

There is nothing new about this; God's plan all along has been for married couples to enter into oneness, not only in a sexual sense[1] but also in a spiritual-relational sense. Indeed, the emphasis in Genesis of two becoming one flesh is on the unity of the couple.[2] This unity can be deepened and enhanced. Thus for the rest of the book, we will focus on practical matters, starting with the topic of how marital oneness plays out in the daily grind.

Oneness as a Matter of Being Present

We once visited a squatter camp in South Africa where tens of thousands of people live daily in dire poverty. What struck me (Sarah) most about their community was not the gagging stench of unburied sewage. It was not the remarkable sight of countless rows and rows of makeshift shanty homes constructed brilliantly of cardboard and cloth. It wasn't even the fact that in each tiny shack there lives approximately twenty-five people. No, what arrested me by far the most was the way that people there are able to be present with one another.

The people in the squatter camp aren't burdened with American preoccupations. Their minds aren't in five places all at once. They aren't thinking about the future or where they're planning to go on their vacation. They aren't thinking about the stock market or wondering if they look okay today. They're just with you. Fully present. One human being with another.

I learned from the people in the squatter camp. I was healed by all the children who swarmed around me. Those little kids showed me for the first time in my life what it feels like to have another person be *with* me. They weren't even talking. In the silence, they just looked at me, encircling me with receptiveness and wide eyes. I didn't have the capacity to absorb their availability. It caught me by such surprise that at one point I burst into tears.

As I look upon that experience, I ask myself sometimes, *Could Jim and I ever learn to be that present with each other? Could we ever come together without lugging along our anxieties or being self-absorbed in subtle ways?* The children who surrounded me were burdened by the poverty they live in, yet freed by their lack of being distracted by the kind of worldly busyness that keeps so many people away from God—and also disrupts their marital dynamic. Indeed, twenty-first century culture in America is a difficult context in which to cultivate oneness in a marriage.

We don't even have kids yet, and we're still too distracted to pay attention to each other in the healing way that those children in South Africa were able to do. We're too fragmented inside. We have not yet learned to entrust ourselves to God enough to let go of our worries and focus on the other one unselfishly.

Entering into oneness takes faith. It also calls for patience. Our friend Tim Lentz made the insightful observation that in marriage, couples have to grow into becoming one flesh. "It's a process," said Tim. "The two shall *become* one flesh." Marriage is hard work because it's hard for two people to become one.

Some marriages, no doubt, seem to run more smoothly than others. I (Jim) don't know exactly why that is. It could be a matter of maturity or having less baggage from the past. Maybe some couples just gel better. Or maybe they blindly sin together and there's only an appearance of gelling. Regardless, you can't truly merge into one if your union is more fleshly than spiritual. Oneness runs deeper than that. Oneness has to do with the spiritual dynamics in the marriage.

Remembering One's Oneness

A very simple way to build oneness in marriage is for the couple to remember who they are. They are one. They are not individually just themselves. When a couple can remember their identity as "one flesh," it changes the way they see themselves. It also changes the way they look at others.

The same principle applies to being a Christian. If you remember your identity in Christ, it changes the way you behave. When I (Jim) remember my identity in Christ, I'm more able to walk in the Spirit and not carry out the desires of my flesh (Galatians 5:16). In the same ways, when I remember my oneness with Sarah, I feel more empowered to be faithful to her and not give in to the deeds of the flesh (Galatians 5:19-21).

When I (Sarah) think of myself as Jim's wife, I tacitly convey that thought to others, even without trying to communicate it. One of the greatest affirmations I've received as a wife happened years ago when a colleague of mine learned that Jim and I were new to our marriage. Incredulously he said, "You've only been married for sixteen or seventeen months?"

"Yeah," I said.

"You're practically a newlywed!" he exclaimed. "That really surprises me. To me, you seem *so* married. I thought you'd been with Jim for ten years."

To this very day, I treasure what my colleague said. I want to come across as being married. I want it to show—in my attitude, in my body language and especially in the way that I relate to other men—that I am committed to Jim. In the very same way, I want to come across as being a

Christian. I want it to be evident in my overall way of life that I am a follower of Christ.

Honoring Wise Boundaries

Another important way to build oneness is to honor wise boundaries in relationships. If a boundary can be defined as a barrier of sorts that keeps the good stuff in and the bad stuff out, then there are two particular boundaries that seem especially important with regard to preserving sexual purity. One applies more to the wife, and the other applies more to the husband. Both boundaries, however, should carefully be honored by both. The first is for the husband not to hide his sexual battles from his wife, and the second is for the wife to dress modestly in public.

Wise boundary number one: Don't hide your sexual battles. It's a boundary issue when a husband makes the choice to exclude his wife from the sexual battle he's facing. Consider 1 John 1:6-9:

> If we say that we have fellowship with Him and yet walk in

the darkness, we lie and do not practice the truth; but if we walk in the Light as He Himself is in the Light, we have fellowship with one another, and the blood of Jesus His Son cleanses us from all sin. If we say that we have no sin, we are deceiving ourselves and the truth is not in us. If we confess our sins, He is faithful and righteous to forgive us our sins and to cleanse us from all unrighteousness.

Walking in the light means not hiding. And yet it's so easy to hide. In the last few decades, for instance, pornography has become pervasive. A man may be minding his own business, when ping!—he's invaded by an advertisement that offers a pornographic picture, just one click away. The same thing can happen to a woman.

It's a costly mistake when the church tells Christian couples not to confess their sexual sins to their spouse. When I (Jim) tell one of my accountability partners about a sexual failure I've had, that's a lot different from telling Sarah. When I confess to her, the feeling of conviction is greater.

There's more sorrow in telling my wife. Godly sorrow leads me to repentance (2 Corinthians 7:10) because not only do I feel grieved before the Lord, but I am then confronted—face to face—with the hurt and a sense of betrayal my wife feels. My accountability partners don't feel the pain that Sarah feels. And while I appreciate their prayers and exhortations, the restorative process is greater when I go directly to Sarah because in entering into her pain I experience, because of our oneness, a deeper pain myself. The reunion we experience empowers me even more to resist the same temptation in the future.

There's no way that men are going to learn how to relate to women just by talking to other men about their problem. There's no way that couples are going to become one in the fullest biblical sense if a husband can't tell his wife what's going on—or vice versa. Husbands need wives, and wives need husbands for help. The church is not going to win the sexual battle unless we, as men and women, band together intentionally as a team.

Of course, we have to be wise. For two or three years my men's group at church thought I was "lucky" to have a wife like Sarah who was spiritually supportive of me and able to accept my confessions. She had a great reputation for being "more mature" than most women. But then one day when I broke faithfulness by watching an episode of *Girls Gone Wild* and confessed to having satisfied myself while lusting for other women, my wife Sarah had a meltdown. I remember her wailing out, "Go ahead and tell your men's group! Sarah lost it!"

Was she crying on behalf of her husband? Was she weeping for me in my defeat? No, she was crying for herself. The more she thought about it, the more she realized that she wasn't merely offended by my betrayal. Her pain was more selfish than that. She was crying because she felt ugly. She felt like the woman on TV was more desirable to me than she was.

So wisdom is called for—I don't confess every specific failure to Sarah. But if I'm headed toward a pattern, telling her can help me turn around.

When accountability from men isn't enough, my friends will sometimes say, "Okay, it's time to tell your wife."

Wise boundary number two: Dress modestly. When a woman is immodest in how she dresses in public, it's a boundary issue. To begin with, however, it needs to be said that women are not to be blamed for men's lust. As the apostle Paul put it, each and every person is to "possess his own vessel in sanctification and honor, not in lustful passion" (1 Thessalonians 4:4-5)—regardless of how a woman is dressed. Jesus could look at women who were dressed immodestly without lusting because Jesus didn't objectify women. The problem of men's lust is a problem of men's hearts; it's not just a problem of women's vanity.

Still, it's imperative for women to be mindful of how vulnerable men can be in their fallen nature. Some men feel they can't even come to church without being sexually tempted by the way some Christian women are dressed. These men feel disappointed because in the one public place where they hope to be released from the battle, they find themselves warring again. Jim has convinced me (Sarah) that immodestly dressed women become stumbling blocks to men far more often than most Christian women might imagine. When Christian women dress immodestly, we break a boundary with the men, and once that boundary is broken, it's difficult for men not to lust—and thereby break a boundary themselves.

Though almost every woman likes to be admired for her looks, her enjoyment suddenly plummets once she starts to put two and two together. When wives start to realize that their *own husbands* are looking at other wives in the same way that men are looking at them, it's suddenly very motivating for wives to be more modest.

One strategy for husbands in fighting this battle is to help the other men by encouraging their own wives to dress modestly. But often husbands resist that kind of strategy:

- "Wearing those kinds of clothes makes my wife feel better about herself. It helps her self-esteem. If

I tell her not to dress like that, it will take away her sense of security."
- "I'm so used to seeing my wife that I don't even notice how she's dressed."
- "I'm proud of my wife's body. I want her to show it off. She looks great."

Our culture has taught women that they don't look pretty unless they're dressed immodestly. Many Christian women have bought into this lie. It's amazing how naive Christian women can sometimes be. In my twenties, I was one of them, so I know. What a woman wants to do is feel pretty. So when a man gives her attention and treats her as if she looks good, she interprets that as personal affirmation. She certainly doesn't tell herself the truth—that she's actually being objectified. Unless the man is overtly creepy, the woman tells herself that she is being appreciated personally.

From the man's point of view, that's not exactly the case. When I have talked to men, they've openly confessed that they're not thinking about the woman's heart or soul. They're thinking about her body. They're thinking about themselves.

See the problem? Women, feeling pretty, are thinking about themselves. And men, feeling lustful, are thinking about themselves. The whole cycle is generated by self-absorption—and it can go either way—with women or men dressing immodestly and men or women doing the lusting. At one evangelical church I watched about sixty women swoon as they talked about their pastor and how good he looks in his tight pants. How are we going to help one another unless we admit that none of us is sexually pure?

Helping Each Other

Too many Christian couples are hesitant to talk about these issues. Many men are convinced that their marriage will fall apart once their wives hear the truth. To some extent this fear is realistic. We know a husband who chose to take a risk by admitting to his wife that he had been struggling with pornography. He confessed to her as an act of contrition. In brokenness, he solicited her support. But as soon as his wife heard, she used that information to blame all of their problems on the husband. Next thing you know, she filed for divorce and left him. Ironically, she lost all trust in her husband right when he was being most honest.

One of the church's greatest needs is for sober-minded wives who can stand in the heat of battle with their husbands. Every Christian husband needs his wife to be his *ezer*—his military helper—with regard to the daily sexual battle. While it's humbling for the wife to face the truth about her husband's sexual weakness, it's also humbling for the husband to admit his sexual weakness to his wife.

I (Sarah) am glad for Jim's candor. Though it bothers me sometimes to think some people might try to scapegoat him by labeling him judgmentally as an "ex-stripper," I trust my husband more because he doesn't hide from me. It's normal for Christians to be tempted sexually. Sexual failings are common, even among the most unlikely people. The more the church denies that, the more difficult it will be for many to experience healing. Part of oneness in the church—and oneness in a marriage—is fighting against sexual sin together.

Building Strong Friendships with People of the Opposite Sex

It might also help the church—and Christian marriages—if people would be less fearful about Christian men and women being friends with one another. We believe in building friendships with the opposite sex. We feel comfortable with this because both of us believe in Christian fellowship.[3]

There truly is a spiritual love that isn't sexual. I (Jim) never experienced this as a nonbeliever. I had closeness with a few of my former girlfriends, but my closeness with them was tainted with sexual sins of our shared pasts. The friendships that I now have with Christian women are ones I never knew were possible. These women are my sisters. There are no sexual overtones in our relationship. Instead, there is ministry and prayer and Christian love. We don't flirt or meet casually or ever get together just to go out. We're friends because we're coministers. It's refreshing in a culture that oversexualizes relationships to have close and loving relationships with women in the Spirit of God.

In his book *The Four Loves,* C.S. Lewis distinguishes friendship from *eros,* sexual love. Friendship is spiritual, not bodily. Unlike lovers who are absorbed in each other, friends are absorbed in some kind of common interest or shared insight. As Lewis phrases it, "We picture lovers face to face, but friends side by side; their eyes look ahead."[4] Whereas *eros* involves naked bodies; friendship has naked personalities. Friendship, unlike *eros,* is idea-oriented, not personally oriented. For the last ten years I (Jim) have worked on a church staff. In a variety of situations, I have worked side by side with Christian women. Especially as a children's pastor, I spent hours colaboring with mothers. As for Sarah, she's worked almost exclusively with men. "You become a man's Friend," says Lewis, "without knowing or caring whether he is married or single... What have all these 'unconcerning things, matters of fact,' to do with the real question, *Do you see the same truth?* In a circle of true friends, each is simply what he [or she] is."[5]

Friendship doesn't threaten sexual love. It is free from the need to be needed. Lewis continues:

> That is why those pathetic people who simply "want friends" can never make any. The very condition of having Friends is that we should want something else besides Friends. Where the truthful answer to the question, *Do you see the same truth?* would be "I see nothing and I don't care about the truth; I only want a Friend," no Friendship can arise.... There would be nothing for the Friendship to be *about;* and Friendship must be about something.[6]

Friendship, so defined, is a relatively unusual relationship. According to Lewis, a great many people never experience it. Some people can't even conceive of it—because of their fallen tendency to sexualize things platonic. In Lewis' words, "Those who cannot conceive Friendship as a substantive love but only as a disguise or elaboration of Eros betray the fact that they have never had a Friend."[7]

The reason Lewis gives of why friendships more seldom occur between men and women is because of the disparity of access.

> Where men are educated and women not, where one sex works and the other idle, or where they do totally different work, they will usually have nothing to be Friends about. But we can easily see that it is this lack, rather than anything in their natures, which excludes Friendship... Hence in a profession (like my own) where men and women work side by side, or in the mission field, or among authors and artists, such Friendship is common.[8]

Being a theologian, I (Sarah) have often been the only woman in a group. For years I was the only female faculty member who served full time in the

Graduate School of Theology at Azusa Pacific University. Before that, I was the only woman student earning a Ph.D. in systematic theology at Trinity Evangelical Divinity School. Still now, I serve on teams in which I'm the only woman. Being friends with men has long been a way of life for me.

Those relationships, however, are categorically different from my marital relationship with Jim. Only Jim is my lover. I hardly ever touch my male friends. We greet one another with a hug sometimes, but basically our friendship is unphysical. A long time ago, I started thinking of my men friends as my brothers. If they happen to be married, I count their wives to be my sisters-in law. That way it doesn't feel awkward whenever I see the wife—because she and I both know that I'm better friends with her husband than I am with her. It's usually expected for siblings to be closer to each other than they are to each other's spouses. So thinking in terms of family really helps.

Prayer helps too. Years ago in my twenties, there was a prominent

Christian man whom I knew felt attracted me. I felt attracted to him too. So I told one of my friends. Upon her instruction, I prayed daily for six months for his marriage to grow deeper and for him to love his wife more than he ever had before. I can't even begin to guess how my prayers may have affected his covenant relationship with his wife. But I do know how my prayers affected me. Not only did my attraction for the man completely fade, but as a result of that test, I learned that sexual temptation can be extinguished in the mind through fervent prayer.

The idea is to honor wise boundaries. Though I often meet with men for coffee or a meal, I never spend time with them casually. I could play golf if we were going out in a group. But that is very different from doing anything that might feel like a date. Ultimately, Jim and I are friends with people we are *able* to be friends with.

If there were someone who had an agenda in pursuing me (Jim), I would withdraw from her and probably even confront her on the issue. Certainly I would tell Sarah about her. If the attraction turned out to be mutual, I would distance myself from the woman and bring the matter into the light of my accountability partners.

If ever I (Sarah) have sensed that there's a mutual attraction between me and someone else, my way of coping has been to tell a woman friend whom I trust to shine light into my heart. I have great friends who are faithful to reprove me and help me stay alert. They're mature enough to be strict and supportive simultaneously. Because of their maturity, I don't have to worry about them blowing my confessions out of proportion. If ever I can tell that I'm starting to entertain any sexually sinful thoughts toward any person in particular, then I know it's time to call one of my girlfriends.

The Husband's Call to Cleave

One of the greatest ways to strengthen marital oneness is for the husband to "cleave" or "be joined" to his wife (Ephesians 5:31). When a husband cleaves to his wife, he is sexually faithful to her. He prioritizes her above his work, above his hobbies, above his family of origin and certainly far above other women.

To cleave is to "be glued to." When a husband cleaves to his wife, he shares his sense of self with her. He sees her as his own body. He does not fall into the trap of dehumanizing her by seeing her as his trophy or possession. When a husband cleaves to his wife, he sees her as a person with her own unique calling from God.

Sometimes Christian men genuinely forget that God calls Christian wives into ministry. I (Sarah) often hear men in seminary make statements such as, "I'm glad my wife can help me with my ministry." They say, "my ministry," as if their wives wouldn't have one without them. The wife's ministry might be different from the husband's, but if she is a Christian, then she has a God-given ministry.

The command to cleave is given by God to husbands. Some Christian men seem tempted to cleave instead to a worldly sense of manhood. A husband may distance himself from his wife for fear that his wife's femininity will somehow make him less of a man. When the quest for manhood becomes a man's absorption, he often falls prey to worldly, unbiblical teaching such as the notion that manhood amounts to "separation." One writer who has influenced evangelicals says, "Becoming a man begins with a break with the mother," but continues throughout life with "a rejection of the feminine."]9]

This is just the opposite of the truth. In the book of Genesis, Eve's femininity accentuated Adam's masculinity. Adam could hardly believe how much like him she was while yet being so mysteriously different. Adam embraced "the feminine" in Eve, understanding that it was a God-given privilege to be closely associated with her. Adam was so exhilarated in the moment he met his wife that he broke out into poetry, saying, "This is now bone of my bones, and flesh of my flesh" (Genesis 2:23).

Adam understood how intimately connected he was to Eve. She was created from his own body. She was "flesh of his flesh" even before they consummated their marriage. After they united physically, the two became one. The miracle of their marriage is that God turned the *same* flesh into *one* flesh. God made them doubly into one.

For this reason, Jesus flashbacked to the Genesis account when the Pharisees asked him, "Is it lawful for a man to divorce his wife for any reason at all?" Instead of simply telling them yes or no, Jesus answered,

> Have you not read that He who created them from the beginning made them male and female, and said, "For this reason a man shall leave his father and mother and be joined to his wife, and the two shall become one flesh"? So they are no longer two, but one flesh. What therefore God has joined together, let no man separate. (Matthew 19:3-6)

The Pharisees asked about divorce, and Jesus told them about creation. In other words, they asked about the law, and Jesus answered them by teaching them instead about God. Knowing that women in first century Jewish culture had no legal rights, Jesus reminded the Pharisees that male *and* female were created by God and that they ultimately share the same origin. God gave Adam his masculine flesh, and yet from it created a woman.

Jesus was helping them understand that it's unthinkable for a husband *not* to cleave to his wife. It's doubly unthinkable for him to divorce her because God has made them doubly one flesh. That's why divorce is so painful: divorce rips the same flesh apart.

Submission and Sacrifice

Another major way to build oneness in a marriage is for the wife to submit to her husband, and the husband to sacrifice himself for the wife.[10] In Ephesians 5:22-25, there is a spiritual parallel between the wife's submission to her husband and the church's submission to Christ, and between the husband self-sacrificial love for his wife and Christ's self-sacrificial love for the church. A great many Christians have been mistaught about these two important parallels.

Instead of being taught the biblical dynamic of oneness—in which the wife submits to her husband, and the husband sacrifices himself for the wife—most have been taught that the wife is to submit *so that* the husband can lead her. Take note: wives are to submit not so that the husband can lead her but so that the two can be one. To submit literally means to "come under." The wife comes under the husband as a body comes under a head.

In a biblical model of marriage, when a wife submits to her husband "as to the Lord," she does not enthrone him as if *he* were her Lord. The husband is not the wife's Lord. The husband is the wife's head. *As an act of obedience to Christ the Lord,* the wife is to submit to her husband as *head* as the church submits to Christ as its head. The wife submits to her husband by coming under him with her support. As the church supports Christ by laboring with him, so the wife supports her husband by laboring with him.

Submission and help go together. It's a huge misunderstanding when people in the church think it's feminine for a woman to be helpless. The wife is the husband's helper *(ezer)*. She was *designed* to give help. God created Eve for the purpose of being helpful to Adam. Adam is the one who needed help; he was "alone," and God said that was "not good" (Genesis 2:18). So when God created woman, she wasn't there to be rescued. She was there to fulfill commandments of God that could not be fulfilled without her help (Genesis 1:28).[11]

Submission has to do with adding to the couple, not subtracting from the wife as a person. When a wife submits to her husband, she does not give up her will. On the contrary, she *exercises* her will to conform her will to her husband's. She does not become a child who obeys him. Rather she chooses, as an adult, to embrace her husband as a means of uniting with him. Submission is not forfeiture. The wife is not commanded to forfeit her perspective or passively give in whenever the couple has a disagreement.

> **Submission has to do with adding to the couple, not subtracting from the wife.**

It is commonly believed that only when a couple is unable to find agreement does the commandment for her to submit become relevant. The problem with this notion of occasional submission is that it fails to meet the standards of the Bible. The Bible says that wives are to be subject to their husbands "in everything" (Ephesians 5:24).

Something similar can be said about the husband's sacrifice. It is often seen to be irrelevant. Countless Christian husbands are under the impression that the commandment counts only in crisis situations when the husband might take a bullet for his wife. The problem with this thinking is that doesn't line up with Scripture. The Bible says for husbands to love their wives just as Christ loved the church and *gave* (past tense) himself up for her (Ephesians 5:25). Christ did more than prepare himself to do something. Christ actually gave himself. He wasn't merely willing to sacrifice his advantage. He really did it. So husbands are to do the same.

In a biblical model of marriage, submission and sacrifice are not optional. They're as necessary in marriage as they are on the ice when a couple is skating together. When a couple is on the ice, the woman entrusts her safety to the controlled strength and care of the man. She submits to him willfully. She cooperates with him by entrusting herself to him as he lifts her and throws her into the air. He, in turn, adjusts himself to her by being sensitive to her. He skates as her partner, not her opponent. Instead of competing with her or overpowering her, he paces with her and features her abilities. As the woman has to submit, so the man has to sacrifice himself in order for the two to perform as one.

In a biblical model of marriage, the wife's submission converges with the husband's sacrifice. Both are ways of cultivating oneness. It's almost counterintuitive, but if you think about it, when the wife comes under the husband, she thereby lifts him up. But then he sacrifices his advantage of being over her by exalting her to where he is. In other words, the husband and wife participate together in a dynamic upward spiral of lifting each other up.

When I (Sarah) speak to people in person, I try to illustrate this simply with my hands. Bringing one hand under the other, I show the wife coming under her husband in submission. Then I move my top hand under the other, showing how the husband sacrifices his advantage and exalts the wife instead. As an act of loving sacrifice, he lifts her up. But then as she submits again, she comes under him again, so up again he goes. But then he chooses again to lift her up again too. As a result, they go up higher and higher together. There is no power struggle. On the contrary, there is genuine trust and love.

In summary, the mystery of marriage is oneness. There are many ways for couples to enhance their marital oneness. The best way is to follow the commandments of Scripture. Once a couple has a vision of their head and body union, they can find creative ways to unite themselves more fully as one flesh.

6

RESOLVING CONFLICT

It's almost hilarious that in all my (Sarah's) years of teaching about the up-up-up dynamic of sacrifice and submission, no one yet has ever asked, "What if the couple reaches an impasse because he wants her to have her way, and she wants him to have his?" That this question never arises says a lot.

Christians are people, and people are very slow to absorb the biblical picture of oneness. The mystery of one flesh so quickly eludes our minds. Even when a couple is in love, they tend to be cautious about the biblical idea of becoming one flesh with their spouse. It's scary to be that vulnerable. Though a couple might embrace the thought of husbandly sacrifice and wifely submission, it's risky to put the thought into practice. Most people wince when it's time to be truly unselfish.

The Biblical Mechanism

It would be magnificent if the relational dynamics of Jim's and my marriage would always yield a head-body, love-respect, sacrifice-submission upward spiral. Many times, however, conversations between the two of us have plunged into the abyss of a head versus body civil war. Though we've always been committed to our marriage, we have nevertheless had our share of fights. But we But we *can't*fight when our hearts are softened toward God. It's only when we choose to turn away from loving God that we turn away from loving each other.

Jesus predicted that people would fight, so he provided a mechanism by which brothers and sisters in Christ could resolve their relational conflicts. This mechanism is a multistep process found in the New Testament. It applies to all Christians in general and thus to married Christians in particular.

Forbearance Before Reproof

First, however, something needs to be said about forbearance. Forbearance is a basic marriage builder. To *forbear* means "to carry or endure." First Corinthians 13 describes forbearance in a number of ways: being slow to anger; not taking into account a wrong suffered; bearing all things; enduring all things.

To forbear means to endure the little quirks and peccadilloes of your spouse. It means to carry the minor pain of being treated imperfectly. It means for spouses to accept each other in their unimproved condition instead of demanding too much too soon.[1] Without forbearance there is no true acceptance from any one person to another. As a principle of practical living, forbearance comes first, before confrontation.

But sometimes forbearance is not enough. Sometimes what is needed is reproof. To reprove means "to expose," to make the special effort to spotlight another person's sin—not out of selfish anger but rather out of love for that person.

To reprove does not mean to be judgmental. It is rather to love someone enough to help them see a sin they might not see. To reprove another person is to offer them a form of relief. It's to grant them special assistance so that they can be delivered from the blindness or hardness of heart that is causing them to be hurtful rather than holy.

Here's how reproof works in a marriage. When your spouse sins against you, and you can't stop feeling offended by it—you can't seem to let it go without distancing yourself emotionally, or feeling sorry for yourself, or complaining to someone else about your partner, or retaliating vindictively in reaction on account of what your spouse did to you, then it is probably time for you to confront.

The Log and the Speck

Confrontation isn't easy when it's done God's way. But it is very redemptive, not only for the person who committed the offense, but also for the one who does the confronting.

The best starting point is found where Jesus says:

> Why do you look at the speck that is in your brother's eye, but do not notice the log that is in your own eye? Or how can you say to your brother, "Let me take the speck out of your eye," and behold, the log is in your own eye. You hypocrite, first take the log out of your own eye, and then you will see clearly to take the speck out of your brother's eye. (Matthew 7:3-5)

This passage reveals the very first step in doing confrontation the biblical way.2 The person who feels offended must "take the log out" of their own eye. That is, whoever feels offended needs to pause and reflect, honestly considering what sin they themselves might have added to the mix.

It's usually wrong to confront your spouse before acknowledging your own sins first. Sometimes the real problem is the log. A log in our own eye can make us *think* there's a speck in the other one's eye when in reality the log has obscured our own vision. Christian confrontations are thus healing for both the person with the log and the person with the speck. Because biblical confrontation is itself an act of love, doing it calls the person to act from a heart of love.

There are two main ways to "take the log out" of your own eye: first, by asking God to show you what your own sin is and then repenting; and second, by preparing yourself spiritually to confront in a Christlike way. Realistically, it might take several hours, or several days, to extricate a log from your own eye. But if you do your part by praying and taking honest inventory of all the many sins you've been forgiven of, it's possible to gain a godly perspective.

> **To hold people accountable Christianly means to speak into their lives for their sake.**

Confrontation should then come not from a self-righteous attitude but rather from a heart of humility. Instead of rushing to nail your spouse for what he or she did to offend you, Jesus says to slow down and examine your own heart first. *Am I harboring resentment against my partner? Am I* for *or* against *my spouse in this situation?* Jesus doesn't want us to sin against our spouse right when we are telling our spouse that they have sinned against us.

To hold people accountable Christianly means to speak into their lives for *their* sake. It means to be *for* them, not against them. In marriage, it means confronting your spouse for the sake of your spouse. It means you're doing this for them, not yourself.

Christian Confrontation

Next step: go to your spouse in private. In Matthew 18:15-17, Jesus offers these instructions to his followers:

> If your brother [or sister] sins, go and show him his fault in private; if he listens to you, you have won your brother. But if he does not listen to you, take one or two more with you, so that by the mouth of two or three witnesses

every fact may be confirmed. If he refuses to listen to them, tell it to the church; and if he refuses to listen even to the church, let him be to you as a Gentile and a tax collector.

Confrontation requires sensitivity. Try not to catch the other person by surprise. If they're in the middle of another activity, wait for better timing. Then reprove them.

As we already know, to *reprove* means "to expose." It does not mean to scold or gripe at. The way to remove a "speck" is first by exposing the problem. Your spouse honestly might not realize what he or she has done. That is not to say the spouse is innocent. The fact might be that your spouse lacks self-awareness. If the spouse does have awareness, but repeated the sin again without remorse, then another round of reproof is needed. Their need is evidenced by the fact that they just sinned against you again.

If, after hearing you, your partner is genuinely sorry, then all is well. The Bible says that "you have won" your spouse (Matthew 18:15). But if he or she is defensive, then it's time to apply the next step.

The most important thing to remember with regard to taking "one or two more with you" (Matthew 18:16) is that you, as the offended party, are the one who gets to decide exactly who those "one or two" will be. The smart thing is to take one or two persons whom your spouse respects; the whole point is to help your spouse to gain the incentive to repent.

If even this step doesn't work, then you take the matter before a larger group of Christians, preferably a group of mature believers. But how are you going to do that unless you're involved in Christian community already? The steps in Matthew 18 are not meant to be applied by people outside the church. How could they be? If they have no fear of Christ, then how could non-Christians be expected to "be subject" to other Christians "in the fear of Christ" (Ephesians 5:21)?

Tragically, many Christians reject the biblical notion of mutual submission. Some don't see the connection between the process described in Matthew 18 and the command given in Ephesians 5:21. Ephesians 5:21, it's assumed, applies only to those who lack authority—"Submit to those in authority" instead of, as Paul wrote it, "Submit to one another." The Matthew 18 process simply doesn't work without submission. The process in Matthew 18 just assumes that you're in touch with other Christians who can serve as "witnesses."

Part of being a Christian is, wherever possible, to be in Christian community. The writer of Hebrews highlights the value of community: "Let us consider how to stimulate one another to love and good deeds, not forsaking our own assembling together, as is the habit of some, but encouraging one another; and all the more as you see the day drawing near" (Hebrews 10:24-25). You can pay a Christian counselor to intervene, but that is not the same as having Christian friends who know you personally in regular life outside of the counselor's office.[3]

The final step outlined in Matthew 18 especially shows that this process is intended for Christians. When telling a larger group still doesn't work, the offender is to be treated as a non-Christian—which is to say they are to be loved evangelistically.

Why Christians Don't Apply Matthew 7 and 18

Many in the church feel threatened by the process of confrontation detailed in Matthew's Gospel. They fear being abused spiritually or being judged or ganged up on—perhaps because that has happened to them in the past.

Invariably less than a tenth of the Christians I (Sarah) have queried have ever participated in a "bring-one-or-two-with-you" event. Why is that? Have we not taken time to read Matthew's Gospel? Have we not been taught to apply the principles in Matthew 7 and 18? Are we unsure whether Jesus' teachings can be applied to our day? The answer could be related to any one of these reasons. Our hesitancies, however, are probably more deep-seated and complex, especially when it comes to applying these biblical principles within marriage. At least five complications come to mind.

First, we're afraid that if we utilize the process given in Matthew 18, our spouses might misunderstand and feel betrayed. They might think we're against them. They might feel unfairly judged. How can a wife invite "one or two others" to join with her as she reproves her husband? Won't he feel ganged up on? Won't he feel disrespected? The fear a spouse can feel is very real. We know women who are scared to death to confront their husbands. We know men who feel just as afraid. It's scary for a husband to "expose" his wife's sins. What if she deprives him after that? What if she badmouths him to the kids? What if she accuses him unfairly?

Second, we might have a faulty view of confrontation. Many people, even Christians, have never seen a positive life-giving confrontation. Thus the whole idea of confronting someone else, to them, seems purely negative. A close friend of mine said when she hears the word *confrontation,* all she can think of is her dad raging at the rest of the family. To her, confrontation means condemnation. It means putting someone else on the spot.

Third, we might disregard Matthew 7 and 18 because following through on Jesus' teachings sounds too time-consuming and inconvenient. Who wants to deal with all the scheduling hassles of arranging for these deep conversations?

Fourth, a number of Christians are skeptical, muttering to themselves, "All this Bible talk about pulling out logs and going to the other person in private is all good and well, but it's never going to work. People are going to do what people are going to do. So why bother?"

Fifth, most of us are missing the fundamental thing that makes applying Jesus' teachings even possible. We simply don't have the right peer pressure. We don't have a Christian culture, so to speak. We have a local church, but the people in our church don't practice Christian values corporately. With the exception of one church, every church I have been part of hardly has any peer pressure in place to practice Matthew 7 and 18.

What, then, can a Christian couple do? To begin with, they can resolve together to follow Jesus Christ to the extent of doing what he says. Sadly to say, many married couples are down-right unwilling to submit themselves to each other for the purpose of applying Matthew 7 and 18. They're afraid to confront each other because they're afraid of being con-fronted themselves.

> **It's not God's way for a husband to be afraid of his wife. It's not God's way for a wife to be fearful of her husband.**

But it's not God's way for a husband to be afraid of his wife. It's not God's way for a wife to be fearful of her husband. Indeed, it's counter to Christianity for spouses to be punitive when their partners try to live by Christian principles. Marriage is a covenant of love, not fear. Love embraces the truth. Love wants to be notified when something goes wrong.

Love doesn't have to be afraid. "There is no fear in love; but perfect love casts out fear, because fear involves punishment, and the one who fears is not perfected in love" (1 John 4:18).

It is wonderful when couples discover what godly confrontation actually looks like. At its best, godly confrontation is life-changing. It's also very bonding. We can attest that to know that your spouse will be faithful to reprove you whenever you get off track is to rest in the security of having a spiritual partner who cares about your character development. We are comrades. We count on each other in our war against sin. We rely on each other in our passionate pursuit of wisdom. We spur each other on to be holy. Day by day we press on together in our mutual quest to be like Christ.

One of my (Sarah's) most longstanding prayers is to pray that I will "love correction." I pray it because I know that I need it. All by myself, I can't remove the speck from my own eye. I wish I could, but I can't. Neither can Jim. Neither can anybody. That's why confrontation is so helpful.

Granted, when people try to confront in a selfishly angry way, all they're really doing is casting judgment. But that explains why Jesus prefaces his remarks in Matthew 7:3-5 with verses 1-2: "Do not judge so that you will not be judged. For in the way you judge, you will be judged; and by your standard of measure, it will be measured to you." Self-righteous judgment (as opposed to sound judgment) is the kind of judgment that says, "My sins don't matter. Only yours do. So I'm here to straighten you out."

Godly confrontation doesn't look like condemnation. It's different. Godly confrontation is others-centered, not self-centered. Orderly, not chaotic. Loving, not abusive. Godly confrontation prohibits shouting matches. It's delicate like surgery, even though it requires great strength.

Maybe we believe in the principles of Matthew 7 and 18 because we have seen them work. With our own eyes, we've seen huge transformations take place. One time in a "bring-one-or-two-with-you" moment, a forty-five year old man (a prominent church leader) broke down in tears and confessed a pattern of sin that he had adamantly denied when he was confronted alone in private.

I (Jim) used to dismiss my sinful outbursts of anger by blaming Sarah. Her private confrontations did nothing to help me take responsibility. For me to experience the appropriate shame in accordance with the conviction of the Holy Spirit, Sarah needed to bring me before two witnesses. To see our friends' affirmation of my offense against Sarah was embarrassing. But the price of momentary embarrassment pales next to the redemptive jolt that led me on the path toward freedom from the imprisonment of my anger. Jesus' system works. I am so thankful Sarah had the courage to love me in this way.

As awful as it might sound to anyone who's never experienced the blessing of Matthew 7 and 18, we can happily assure you that the dread of it is far, far worse than the reality. Though the process of being reproved in the company of witnesses is humbling, even embarrassing, the effects of it are awesome and worthwhile. I (Sarah) remember when Jim told our Christian friends about me and my reactive sarcasm. I just sat there in the spotlight being exposed. There was no place to run, no place to hide, because if I tried to weasel out, it would only underscore Jim's point. I feel relieved to have repented from a measure of my sin. I am blessed to be unburdened by the sins that others have helped me to eliminate from my life. I can confidently say that I'm not stuck in any sin because Jim and other people are helping me to make progress. Jim and I won't let each other stay stuck. We refuse to give in to sin's inertia. We refuse to give up and say about one another, "Well, that's just Jim. That's just Sarah. Don't expect anything better."

We have hope because of Matthew 7 and 18. We have hope because the Holy Spirit of God is alive and well. We have hope because God who began a good work in us "will perfect it until the day of Christ Jesus" (Philippians 1:6).

This whole process is love playing out. It's beautiful to hear your spouse saying, "I am here to help you be like Jesus. I am here to remind you of your dignity and calling. I am here to applaud when you dare to be loved in the deepest kind of way by your Maker." God doesn't want us to be stranded in sin. God doesn't want us to miss out on his liberating grace.

A good thing for a couple to do is decide in advance how they would like to be approached the next time they are the "offender." We have coached each other to say, "Honey, I know you care about the way you relate to me and that you're trying to be more Christlike. (Pause.) There was a moment earlier today when it seemed like you didn't notice what you did to me. Is this a good time for us to talk?"

It's important for couples to be convinced that living out the Scriptures is *not* too big of a hassle, especially when we remember what's at stake. The grand result of our failure to take time to "take the speck out" from our spouse's eye is this: the speck stays lodged. The speck—the bad habit—the unconfessed sin—prevails unless we labor to get it out.

And guess who sees it? Our kids see it. Non-Christians see it. They see the speck. And because so many Christians aren't sorry about those specks, we appear as hypocrites in the world. Almost everyone agrees that the number one critique that nonChristians constantly hurl against the church is our hypocrisy—our unremoved logs and specks. The day Christians get serious about doing our needed "eye-cleaning" will be the day that some of our dearest loved ones come to Christ and many hurting marriages get healed.

When the Marriage Is Bleeding

Sometimes, however, Christian couples can't access Matthew 7 or 18, much less 1 Corinthians 13 with its appeal to forbearance because all they can do is fight. Their every conversation quickly morphs into another heated battle. As soon as they open their mouths, multiple offenses surface on both sides. He is hurt, and she is hurt. Both feel accused and misunderstood.

Every attempt at a rational exchange collapses into another round of war.

We went through this early in our marriage. We got professional counseling, paying someone to play referee because we couldn't stay in the game without fouling each other. Both of us were angry, and both of us were hurt. Back then, we didn't see how our very different backgrounds had taught us very different ways of coping with relational problems. We really didn't know each other well. We thought we knew each other, but we didn't to the extent of being able to represent each other's side. I (Jim) knew what I thought, and I knew what I thought Sarah thought, but I really didn't know her perspective. Likewise, she knew what she thought, and she knew what she thought I thought, but she really couldn't articulate my view.

Back then we didn't grasp the full significance of our different personalities. Because we're generally so compatible, we underestimated the significance of our differences. We didn't realize, for instance, the major clash between Sarah's intuitive way of thinking and my sensory way of thinking until about three years into our marriage when we compared our test results of the Meyers-Briggs personality profile. Once we understood how challenging it can be for an intuitive person (who thinks in terms of the big picture and abstract thoughts) and a sensory person (who thinks in terms details and concrete facts) to communicate effectively, we could better appreciate the validity of each other's viewpoints. Today we understand that Sarah tends to be more conceptual and integrative in her thinking whereas I tend to view things more discretely as they are in the present context. More will be said about that in chapter nine.

It's hard when a couple truly gets psyched out (as we were) by each other's peculiar coping mechanisms. When reality feels harsh and overwhelming, I tend to be pessimistic and cynical. Sarah, by contrast, becomes all the more determined to be fiercely optimistic by kicking into her "try harder" mode. So when our fights would persist, I would feel hopeless, and Sarah would feel threatened by my hopelessness and then try to manipulate me. She brought huge amounts of energy to our arguments. Whereas I felt exhausted by the intensity of our fights, Sarah seemed indefatigable. She honestly believed that if we would just hang in there and endure another hour of a destructive conversation, things would eventually get better. To me, the truth was evident: we were worms.

I (Sarah) used to hate it when Jim would label us as "worms." At night sometimes when we were laying in bed he would literally start announcing, "We're worms! We're worms!" He saw us as fallen creatures, stricken and tormented, pitifully consigned to futility. Any hopeful signs that were brought to his attention were summarily dismissed as fleeting and illusory. Jim thought I was fatally idealistic.

We can laugh about it now, but at the time it wasn't funny. Our marriage was hemorrhaging. The pain of the past had encroached into our marriage and caused us to lose perspective. We had so many expectations, so many hot buttons, so many emotional disappointments. We loved each other, but we couldn't go three days without quarreling. We wanted to be together, but we couldn't be together without fighting. We couldn't find a way to communicate without hurting each other's feelings.

So we got help. We found a counselor through our church who gave us wordless ways of communicating. Once he invited us to become a living a sculpture right there in his office. He told us to position ourselves bodily in a way that illustrated how we felt in relation to each other. The counselor made me go first, so I directed Jim to crouch over me in a way that showed how I felt bullied and crushed. Then Jim directed me to a position that showed how lacerated and ripped apart he felt. Both of us were stunned by the exercise.

The other assignment the counselor gave was something we implemented over the next several months. It helped us by far more than anything. The counselor told Jim to place his hand on my heart and silently pray for me. After he finished, I was instructed to do the same for Jim. Then our counselor told us to do that every night.

Regardless of what happened in any given day, at night after quieting down, we were supposed to pray for each other with a hand physically placed on the other's heart. So every night I would place my hand on Jim and pray until my heart felt softened. Sometimes I would pray for thirty minutes. Then I would roll back toward my side of the bed and wait for Jim to place his hand on me.

I (Jim) did it the first night after we went to counseling. I did it sporadically again the next week. But since it didn't serve as a cure-all to our marriage, I gave up. I stopped doing it altogether. Night after night, Sarah would pray for me, and I wouldn't pray for her at all. She cried herself to sleep almost every time the disappointment happened. Still, I would just lay there. Both of us would lay there in the silence. It took weeks for me to experience a change of heart.

It was hard because I (Sarah) was so reactive during the day. I cannot describe what a turning point it was the night that Jim leaned over and touched me. For five months after that, every night we both prayed for each other in silence taking turns placing our hands on each other's heart. Then something happened that surprised me. After all those months, Jim began to pray out loud. He broke the sacred silence that had incubated our marriage. He broke it by invoking Almighty God. The whole room was filled with Jim's prayer. Our marriage had stopped bleeding. Both of us had experienced transformation.

Waiting for the Oak Tree to Grow

During the season of our silent prayer times, I (Sarah) was washing the dishes one day and looking out the window at a fledgling little oak tree outside. It had tiny little twigs and sparsely distributed leaves. There was really no trunk to speak of. The tree looked more like a stick.

That's our marriage, I thought to myself. But before I could descend into self-pity, I sensed the Lord saying to me, "That's right. That's your marriage for now. But if you'll be patient and keep depending on me, your marriage is going to grow into a beautiful big oak tree that will weather many storms and last for many years to come."

I wish I could say that our marriage reached a tipping point after which everything was better. But that is not what happened. Our growth was incremental, not catastrophic. Though we stopped going to counseling, we kept meeting with other couples from church. Jim, moreover, went to anger class. He mastered the material by going through the class three times.

Over the next few years, our fights still escalated, but not as frequently or intensely. What kept us reeled in was communion. Every time we partook of the body and blood of Christ, we remembered God's grace once again. It's a privilege to be invited to the Lord's Supper. Through communion we receive "true food" and "true drink" (John 6:55), and we partake of the "new covenant" of God's forgiveness in Christ Jesus (Luke 22:20).

For us, the Lord's Supper is a meal that offers healing to our marriage. As we physically hold the bread, remembering Christ's body and blood, and physically hold the cup, remembering Christ's spilled blood, we become remorseful for our sin. Before we bring the bread to our mouths or put the juice to our lips, we pause long enough to apologize to each other and pledge our love again with new resolve. Clarity of mind regarding our own sin comes to us best at the Lord's table. When we focus on Christ, we see our own sin, not each other's anymore.

We love our local church, New Song, because communion time there is unhurried. We have about fifteen or twenty minutes to worship through taking communion. It is normal at our church during communion time to see people praying with each other and wiping tears.

I (Jim) remember one Sunday morning, sitting frozen, my eyes fixed on the cup and the color of blood that filled it. I imagined the cross drenched by the blood of my Savior. Then I looked at the unleavened bread with its holes and stripes. It reminded me of Christ's body, brutally beaten.

My eyesight became blurred as a tear rolled down my cheek into the palm of my hand. How could I partake of the elements in celebration of my forgiveness of sins when I sat so consumed in unforgiveness? My heart was hardened. I had spoken vile words to Sarah that Sunday morning. Still, anger coursed through my veins. I stiffened my neck, refusing to let go of my pain.

With the elements still in my hands, the Spirit came upon me, and I broke. Many tears were washing my cheeks. The conviction of the Holy Spirit pierced my sin-stained heart as I cried out to the Lord for forgiveness. I could not continue to hold back. I turned to my wife sitting next to me and saw the mirror image of my experience happening also to her. In our eagerness to confess our own sins, we spoke simultaneously with words born out of contrition. The wedge between us was ripped like a veil—as the curtain in the temple was suddenly rent the moment Jesus bowed his head and died.

Taking communion infuses our marriage with grace. We start with a clean slate every time we share the Lord's meal. Resolving marital conflict seems petty to us in light of the great conflict that Christ resolved between sinners and God when he laid down his life on our behalf. Resolving conflict in marriage is difficult work, but because of Christ's work on the cross, a husband and wife can find the power to forgive and the commitment to keep growing in oneness, even if the conflict recurs.

7

DEFINING EXPECTATIONS

Under every single fight we've ever had lay at least one selfish expectation. For example, early in our marriage I (Sarah) had the expectation that when Jim came home from doing landscaping work, he would want to kiss as soon as he walked in the door. I knew he was tired from long hours in the weather doing hard physical labor, but since my preferred way of communicating love is to be affectionate, it didn't occur to me that he might want some space instead. As soon as I heard his car pulling into the driveway, my heart would start to flutter with excitement. With great anticipation I would drop whatever I was doing and rush to the door and stand there with this giant expectation. From my point of view, this was an appointed time for romance. From Jim's view, it was an appointed time to take a hot shower. Jim felt dirty, stinky and exhausted. He just wanted to get cleaned up, eat some dinner, and go to sleep.

Several months later we were sitting in the office of a Christian marriage counselor, telling him the details of my devastation, Jim's reaction, my reaction to his reaction, his reaction to mine, and how we spiraled through that fight with full drama and histrionics ten or twelve times a month.

Jim was adamant. "She's got this expectation."

After listening to our story, the counselor rubbed his chin and responded in an understated tone, "Are you sure she's the only one?"

Sarah and I exchanged quick glances.

"Do you expect the same privacy, Jim, that you had when you were single? Aren't you *expecting* Sarah to leave you alone until you're ready to interact and be social?"

What we learned from that counselor was that both of us had selfish expectations. Both of us were driven by two little words: "I want."

"I (Sarah) want romance."
"I (Jim) want space."
"I (Sarah) want love."
"I (Jim) want respect."

Selfish expectations quench the Holy Spirit. They war against God by enthroning dark desires of the self. What I selfishly expect becomes that which I selfishly demand. "I want. I expect. I demand. And if I don't get my way, I'll react."

Nobody likes it when someone else reacts. Reactions, by definition, are destructive. To react is to follow a selfish impulse. To react is to evade responsibility. To react is to dismiss—with irrational abandon—the present opportunity to respond with consideration and wisdom.

Sarah's usual way of reacting is to overdramatize and be sarcastic. My (Jim's) usual way is to blame—and I blame Adam for this.

It's easy to imagine where our marital fights go when both of us start reacting. I blame, and Sarah reacts by going on and on about how "innocent" I am and how inspiring it is for her to "behold a living specimen of perfection." Then I blow up, and then she torments me by mouthing off a litany of disingenuous confessions of all her "woeful guilt" when she and I both know that she's furious at me for dumping my issues on her.

A few years into our marriage, we went back to marriage counseling, this time in California instead of Chicago. On the first or second session, our counselor called us "Nitro and Glycerin." He told us we were two rams bashing horns. At the bottom of our problem of negotiating boundaries was a problem of competing expectations.

The counselor looked at Sarah and said, "You *think* you're mad at Jim for distancing himself emotionally from you, but that's part of your attraction to him. You didn't get that kind of space in your family growing up. You're relieved to have that space. You need the kind of space Jim offers."

With the same level of expertise, he said to me, "Jim, you *think* you're mad at Sarah for pursuing you emotionally and refusing to back down when you reject her, but that's part of your attraction to her. You don't have experience being intimate. What Sarah is trying to give is the very thing you want most."

Both of us were stunned again. It was the greatest "who'd a thunk it" moment of our marriage. We talked about it all the way home.

Blinded to Our Selfish Expectations

It is common to be blind to the fact that we're reacting due to unmet expectations. Most people's tendency is to justify their reaction based on what the other person did. Consequently, most people stay blind. Even as Christians, we often remain blind to what we're doing. Too often we don't see that we ourselves are guilty of bringing selfish expectations into the mix. It's hard to see the truth—because everything happens so fast when relational dynamics play out. Before you know it, another expectation has invaded.

"I already told you that!" snaps the wife who expects her husband to hear her the first time.

"Man, you're crabby!" says the husband who expects to be honored by his wife.

"I just wish you'd pay attention," says the wife, still expecting from her husband.

"I just wish you'd be polite," says the husband, still expecting from his wife.

Selfish expectations can make a nice person mean. They can warp a personality in a second. Selfish expectations can be violent, even lethal. Selfish expectations are hostile to God because they idolize the self and its wants.

Paul told the Galatians, "If you bite and devour one another, take care that you are not consumed by one another" (Galatians 5:15). We went to counseling because we knew we were devouring one another. In spite of the fact that the theme of our marriage is "rooted and grounded in love" (Ephesians 3:17), we were biting one another, almost consuming one another, because we were being controlled by our selfish expectations, and selfish expectations are rooted and grounded in greed.

Selfish expectations, as we have found out, can be misleading. At the very deepest level, people don't always want what people *think* they want. I (Sarah) thought I wanted a lovey-dovey husband who would saturate me with kisses, but really I want the assurance of Jim's love. While I do long for affection from my husband, the counselor was right—I also want space from Jim. Space so I can write. Space so I can travel. Space so I can wear the leadership mantle of my calling.

Conversely, I (Jim) was under the impression that I wanted a Christian wife who was so accepting of me that she wouldn't try to prod me to be intimate and vulnerable emotionally. But what I really want is to be known. I want Sarah to know me through and through. One of my mantras to Sarah is "Know your husband."

Paul the apostle said something to the Galatians that relates to the challenge of managing expectations. He said, "Walk by the Spirit, and you will not carry out the desire of the flesh" (Galatians 5:16). That is, walk by the Spirit, so that you can be a husband, so that you can be a wife, who truthfully can say, "The Lord is my shepherd, I shall not want" (Psalm 23:1).

Selfish expectations are subtle forms of want that feed on insecurity and greed. We want because we're nervous. We want because we somehow feel deprived. We want because we're entitled.

Selfish expectations can play out in a variety of ways. Many people, for example, place unrealistic expectations on themselves. After I (Jim) became a Christian, I thought I would be able to repent from *every* sin now that I was numbered with the saints. My expectation was selfish because I didn't want to learn to walk by faith. I wanted the Christian life to be easier than it is. There were times when I became disillusioned, even angry at God, because my selfish expectations lied to me.

How many Christians can relate to that struggle? How many of us expect too much greatness from ourselves and far too little from God? How commonplace is it for genuine Christians full of selfish expectations to feel too embarrassed to admit the actual truth of who they are?

One time we were arguing, both feeling furious and hurt. Dramatically I (Sarah) dashed into the guest bedroom to wail and pray to God. I went back and forth from praying on my knees to writhing on the floor in anguish. I marinated myself in self-pity. I felt so sorry for myself because I had a steely husband who kept telling me that I was immature. I expected my husband to be my comforter, not my indicter. But Jim is a prophet. He calls out the sin, even when he sees it in his wife.

I remember crying to God, "He's so cold! He's so hardened! Please hold me together and help me to get through this!" Then I rolled back on the floor to continue my gnashing of teeth.

Right then, Jim opened the bedroom door. I almost couldn't believe it. My iron-willed husband had finally—for the first time since I'd met him—come to my rescue. How long I had awaited that dear moment. With his crystal blue eyes, he looked at me piercingly and said, "Sarah Sumner, you're the most capable woman I have ever met in my life. What are you doing on the floor?" Two seconds later, he closed the door and left.

Talk about unmet expectations. I couldn't have felt sorrier for myself. Repositioning myself on my knees, I said out loud to God, "Heartless! See! He's heartless!" Then I buried my face in my hands.

That's when God chimed in. The Lord said to me very gently, "I see Jim's rough edges. But I am using Jim to shape your character. He's right about you being immature."

I remember thinking to myself, *What? Even God is on Jim's side? I can't believe this!*

Then God continued, "And, Sarah, I'm answering your prayers. For years you have prayed that I would make you a vessel of honor in my kingdom. You have poured out your heart, begging me to grow you, groom you, take you, fill you, use you. And I have heard your prayers. You're not the most capable woman in the world, but you do have a calling on your life, and I, the Caller, am preparing you to do my work. Jim is a chosen instrument in my hand."

Overcoming Selfish Expectations

In order to break the cycle of selfish expectations, we have to slow down and slow-motion the situation. We have to pay attention to our inner motivations, so that we can become more self-aware. In other words, to overcome the power of selfish expectations, we have to make the effort to acknowledge them. This requires humility.

It's hard to admit how selfish our expectations sometimes are. Though most people have the goodwill to have positive expectations on behalf of other people, we are usually not insulted when other people are let down. We might be sad for them, and at times we may react protectively, but not with the same force that we do with regard to ourselves. If someone else, for instance, misses their next plane due to an airline's inefficiency, most of us don't have trouble staying calm. Likewise, if someone else gets sick, most of us don't find ourselves reacting as a result. But if *we ourselves* get sick or if we have to miss something that we've been looking forward to, we might be found complaining.

Once selfish expectations are acknowledged, they can be more easily surrendered. In a recent conversation, I (Jim) was telling Sarah a story about something that went wrong at work. What I wanted was her comfort. But what I got was a cognitive response. Just as I was starting to react, I caught myself midstream and realized that I had an expectation. We avoided a skirmish as I halted myself, collected my thoughts, and gently explained that I had hoped for an empathic response. I didn't blame her for being insensitive. I merely tried to help her see why I had been tempted to react. That was a victory moment in our marriage.

Here's the lesson in this: You have to die to yourself. The apostle Paul put it more severely: "You fool! That which you sow does not come to life unless it dies" (1 Corinthians 15:36). Christ beckons us to die because he wants us to experience new life. Even as Christians, we are going to struggle with selfish expectations. The plan, however, is for Christians to have healthy and holy expectations—not selfish expectations.

Healthy expectations are byproducts of trust. Because I (Jim) *trust* Sarah to tell me the truth, I *expect* her to tell me the truth. That expectation is not selfish. Selfish expectations serve the self alone. Healthy expectations serve the community. Healthy expectations include all kinds of things such as expecting the FDA to inspect our meat, expecting public bridges to be sturdy, expecting teachers to be literate, expecting young people to want to get married, expecting children to want to grow up, expecting teenagers to gather with their friends, and so forth.

By contrast, holy expectations are limited to people who trust God. It is only by faith that anyone can say with integrity, as the prophet Micah did:

> But as for me, I will watch
> expectantly for the Lord;

> I will wait for the God of my salvation
> My God will hear me.
>
> Do not rejoice over me, O my enemy
> Though I fall I will rise;
> Though I dwell in darkness, the lord is a light for me. (Micah 7:7-8)

It takes faith to watch expectantly for the Lord. It takes faith to believe that God will act. It takes faith to be assured that God listens. Only the heart of faith confidently knows that God is a light in the darkness.

Holy expectations, unlike selfish expectations, make a person more emboldened and resilient. By virtue of his holy expectations, the apostle Paul was able to suffer and endure a multitude of afflictions without feeling sorry for himself. Three times Paul was beaten. Once he was stoned. Three times he was shipwrecked. A night and a day he spent in the deep. He experienced dangers from rivers, dangers from robbers, dangers from his countrymen, dangers from the Gentiles, dangers in the city, dangers in the wilderness, dangers on the sea, dangers among false brethren. He was in labor and hardship. He went through many sleepless nights. He was in hunger and thirst. He was often without food, often in cold and exposure. In addition to all that, he was burdened everyday by the pressure he felt because of his concern for all the churches (2 Corinthias 11:23-28). Paul had a mindset of faith. He told the Philippians:

> For I know that this will turn out for my deliverance through your prayers and the provision of the Spirit of Jesus Christ, according to my earnest expectation and hope, that I will not be put to shame in anything, but that with all boldness, Christ will even now, as always, be exalted in my body, whether by life or by death. For to me, to live is Christ and to die is gain. (Philippians 1:19-21)

To expect the Lord Jesus to be exalted in our bodies, to expect that kind of honor, to believe that we cannot be put to shame, to truly *know that* is profoundly liberating. On account of God's faithfulness, holy expectations are never unmet—so we don't have to worry about reacting to them. We might selfishly react when the *timing* of the fulfillment of God's promises doesn't suit us or when we don't approve of *how* God decides to act. But when that happens, it's the selfish expectation that fails us. Holy expectations are related to the hope we have in Christ. Holy expectations are unfailing because they're anchored in the truth of God.

> **As Christians, we are called to sanctify our marriages by letting go of selfish expectations, holding on loosely to healthy expectations and hanging on to holy expectations.**

As Christians, we are called to sanctify our marriages by letting go of selfish expectations, holding on loosely to healthy expectations and hanging on to holy expectations. For me (Sarah) to expect Jim to be affectionate in my timing and on my terms is for me to set myself up to be reactive. It's a selfish expectation. It *is* fair for me, as Jim's wife, to expect him to be affectionate in our marriage. That's a healthy expectation. It's not healthy, however, for me to react when my healthy expectation is unmet.

Jesus calls us to a standard that simply can't be met apart from the power of the Holy Spirit. He said, "Love your enemies, and do good, and lend, expecting nothing in return; and your reward will be great, and you will be sons of the Most High; for He Himself is kind to ungrateful and evil men" (Luke 6:35). If we are to love our enemies—and expect nothing from them in return—how much more are we to love our spouse?

When we earnestly expect God to help us and diligently look to him for his help, we can enter into the freedom of true love. Love is patient when our spouse is sinning. Love is kind when our spouse is being rude. Love doesn't live by selfish expectations because love does not seek its own (1 Corinthians 13:4-5).

Psychologist William James, a non-Christian, produced a formula for happiness.

Happiness = Performance/Expectation

The formula suggests there are two ways for people to increase their happiness in relationships: (1) increase performance or (2) decrease expectations. Recast in terms of Christian love, the formula says to increase performance by serving other people through love, and decrease expectations by dying to yourself, so that you won't be demanding or reactive. Listen to the words of the apostle Paul:

> But through love serve one another. For the whole Law is fulfilled in one word, in the statement, "You shall love your neighbor as yourself." But if you bite and devour one another, take care that you are not consumed by one another. But I say, walk by the Spirit, and you will not carry out the desire of the flesh. (Galatians 5:13-16)

It's axiomatic that no one can control another person. I (Jim) cannot control Sarah or alter her performance in our marriage. But I can control myself and make changes in myself. By the power of God, I can be miraculously renewed, and so can Sarah. We can be transformed by the Holy Spirit such that we no longer expect the things we used to.

A good way to judge if you're reacting or not is to ask yourself the question: *Am I bearing the fruit of the Spirit when my expectations are unfulfilled?* The fruit of the Spirit is love, joy, peace, patience, kindness, goodness, faithfulness, gentleness, self-control (Galatians 5:22-23). Responding with the fruit of the Spirit is the very best way to increase performance.

By the way, we got the greeting-at-the-door thing figured out.

Lowering Expectations Without Lowering Christian Standards

There's one important question that begs to be addressed before we move on to the next chapter. How do we, as Christians, lower the expectations that we place upon our spouse without compromising the holiness of God's standards? We don't want to enable our spouse's bad habits. Nor do we want to fail to do our part to help our spouse become a better person.

The whole Bible is relevant to the subject of expectations, but three important truths correlate with three important promises. First, God has made it known that every human being, with the exception of Jesus Christ, is a sinner. Romans 3:10 says it starkly: "There is none righteous, not even one." From this we should know to expect our spouse, even our Christian spouse, to be unrighteous. The Word of God forewarns us—sinners are going to sin. If I (Sarah) can bear in mind that both Jim and I are sinners, I stand a better chance of adjusting my expectations accordingly. The promise of God is this: "He who began a good work in you will perfect it until the day of Christ Jesus" (Philippians 1:6). Yes, we are sinners. But there is hope for us because God is changing us, conforming us into the image of Christ Jesus. Part of the way God is changing us is by sharpening us through each other.

One of the most helpful ways to think about adjusting your expectations is to forgive your spouse before they sin. Henri Nouwen used to say it with such authority: "Forgiveness is to allow the other person *not* to be God!"

Second, Jesus made it plain: "In the world you have tribulation" (John 16:33). In a sense we are naive, and in another sense we are rebellious, when we refuse to come to grips with the unflattering naked truth that life is hard. The world and everything in it is broken. Although the beauty of creation and the dignity of people have been somewhat left intact, both are also marred. On earth tribulation is a given. Catastrophes will happen. Mistakes will be made. Utopian plans for Babel will not prosper.

Selfishly we don't want to face tribulation. We would rather be exceptions, people who are exempt from that hard truth. But if we fail to embrace the first part of Jesus' statement, "In the world you have tribulation," we end up making light of the second part, "but take courage; I have overcome the world" (John 16:33). Practically that means when we hesitate to accept that tribulation is inevitable, we thereby reject the joy that is supposed to be ours. Instead of being joyful in our earthly tribulations, too often we react in anger and self-pity. Too often we react by venting our pain on our spouse.

The ultimate truth of any trying situation is that Christ has already overcome it. Because Christ has overpowered all the evil in the world, we can rest assured that even in our grief, we can also be of good cheer.

Third, the Word of God reveals that aging is a predictable phenomenon. In 2 Corinthians 4:16, Paul declares that outwardly we are "decaying." The process of aging is humbling. Sometimes people feel assaulted by the gradual aging process. Aging can be scary and unsettling. In marriage, it can be difficult to accept the aging process of our spouse. A husband wants his wife to have the same good-looking figure that she had before childbirth or menopause. A wife wants her husband not to smell like an old man. Both expect the other to accept them in their frailty, and yet both have a propensity to be critical.

It's easy to overlook the hidden grace that is embedded in our wrinkles. We forget that outward signs of bodily decay actually provide empirical evidence that we, as believers, "inwardly ... are being renewed" (2 Corinthians 4:16 NIV).

Reality Promises

1. Every person is a sinner. (Philippians 1:6)
2. In the world you will have tribulation. (John 16:33)
3. People age as they grow older. (2 Corinthians 4:16)

Holy expectations revitalize and strengthen Christian marriages by reminding us of the truth of the world's great need for Christ. Holy expectations humbly accept reality while clinging to the promises of God. The more a Christian couple can adjust their expectations, the more they can live as one in Christ.

8
HOT BUTTON ISSUES

Everyone has hot buttons. One way to discern what your hot buttons are is to watch and see what triggers you to react. Body image, for instance, is a common hot button for people. We may roll with other punches, but when it comes to what is said about us physically, we can become hypersensitive.

I (Sarah) tend to have a hot button about my looks. Not my makeup, but the features of my figure and my face. There are reasons for my personal insecurities. I've worked hard through those, and I've experienced a number of breakthroughs. But still, I'm not as settled as I'd like to be.

Jim, by contrast, feels fine about his looks. In fact, people marvel at how comfortable Jim is with his body. (Little do they know Jim's background.) To give you an idea, in September 2006 to celebrate our church's twentieth anniversary, the drama team made a "Then and Now" video to show what people looked like in the 1980s compared to today. Though people were entertained throughout the film, they roared out loud with laughter when they saw Jim's pictures.

His "Then" shot featured him, young and tan, standing against a fence wearing Levi's and no shirt. His stomach was virtually fatless, his arms disproportionately built-up. His chest was defined by sculpted V-cut muscles. His face was chiseled and rugged, and his countenance too cool to hint of a grin. To accentuate his manliness, he had a cowboy-like bandana around his neck.

For his "Now" picture, he made a parody of himself by mimicking the same scenario. There he was twenty-five pounds later, no V-cut, no tan, and an exaggerated look of being cool. The main feature of the photo was his bloated beach ball belly that he theatrically stuck out as much as could. He still wore the cowboy-like bandana, but somehow it had lost its effect because his pectorals were soft and flabby; his chest hair slightly grayed, and his face subtly framed by a double chin.

After the party I don't know how many men took the initiative to tell Jim, "I would never be able to do that." They said they'd be too embarrassed. For them it was too much to expose their middle-aged fat or laugh at their fading sex appeal.[1]

Babies aren't self-conscious about their bodies. Preschool children aren't ashamed of the way they look. It's people who are older—people who have been hurt. That's what hot buttons are about. They're about past hurts. Festering unhealed wounds. Unresolved issues that are painful to come to terms with or address.

In marriage hot button issues inevitably come out. They may come out of nowhere at certain times. One trigger is the pain of feeling ugly. Another is the pain of feeling useless. Still another is the pain of feeling stupid. Yet another is the pain of being rejected or overlooked or unappreciated.

Couples will benefit greatly if they learn how to love each other in their hot buttons. It's healing to a marriage if one can show compassion even when the other one is reacting. People need compassion often when they're most difficult to love. Spouses need compassion, even if it at times they don't deserve it.

Compassion literally means to "suffer with." I (Jim) might be irritable, for instance, angry at myself for having said something that I thought made me look stupid. In my irritability, I might be harsh with Sarah. If she personalizes my harshness and interprets the situation with an eye to herself, she will probably react. But if she pauses long enough to find out what I'm facing and then makes a conscious decision to empathize with me and forego defending herself, then she can "suffer with" me by showing compassion.

At some point, however, people need correction. Husbands need correction, and wives need correction. People do better when we are exhorted and reproved and rebuked in loving ways (2 Timothy 4:2). From experience we know that if we resist correction, then we are going to stay stuck. But if we become receptive to our spouse's loving correction, then we can "excel still more" (1 Thessalonians 4:1).

Finding Freedom from Our Hot Buttons

In Christ it is possible for people to change for the better. Longstanding negative patterns can be changed into positive ones. Hot buttons can be cooled. The fire that fuels the flames of defensiveness can be smothered—but only by one thing: truth.

Truth alone can set people free. Compassion doesn't have that power. Compassion soothes the pain; compassion softens the heart; compassion is essential to the Christian life. But compassion doesn't set people free. Jesus said, "You will know the truth, and the truth will make you free" (John 8:32). Truth uniquely can liberate people from the lies that keep us in bondage.

Truth without compassion though is not entirely truthful because it fails to represent the nature of God. It's not God's way to push the truth on other people without taking into account their vulnerabilities. God is a God of truth *and* compassion. Thus the Scriptures say to "[speak] the truth in love" (Ephesians 4:15). The way to deal with hot buttons is to be both truthful and compassionate. Compassion and truth are meant to go together. Compassion cushions people so that truth can do its work.

Hot buttons are symptomatic; they are not representative of a person's inner core. If a husband says to his wife with regard to one of his hot buttons, "Look, this is who I am, and you're going to have to learn to accept that," he is choosing irresponsibility. He is pressuring his wife to excuse his destructive behavior. What the husband needs to realize is that his outward behavior, though reflective of his character, is *not* part of who he has to be.

If a husband becomes irritable and sarcastic whenever his wife asks him to help her around the house, he may do this for at least two reasons: (1) he feels as though his efforts are futile since his wife nearly always complains about how he works; (2) he feels exempt from doing housework.

Regardless of how a couple divides their chores, it is sinful—and inexcusable—for a husband to be irritable and sarcastic. If in self-defense he intimidates his wife by saying, "Hey, back off! You know this is a hot button for me," then he is copping out. He is refusing to take responsibility and change. He stays trapped *in the pride* that causes him to be irritable and sarcastic, and he stays caught *in the lie* that tells him that his efforts are useless.

How can this husband be set free? By embracing the truth about his sin, and by exercising the courage to turn away from the lie that's in his head, and by entering into godly sorrow.

By embracing the truth about his sin. To begin with, the husband needs to learn to own his own sin and not deny that it comes from his own heart. Jesus said, "There is nothing outside the man which can defile him if it goes into him; but the things which proceed out of the man [out of the heart] are what defile the man" (Mark 7:15; see also 7:21).

By exercising the courage to turn away from the lie that's in his head. When the wife derides the husband's contribution to the housework, what he hears her saying is, "You're useless. You're no help at all." Undoubtedly, that's a lie. But the key is for the husband to *realize* that's a lie—to take responsibility for reacting to that statement, or rather to his perception that the statement was made by his wife.

Assume the wife *didn't* really say to him, "You're useless!" Assume that instead it was the husband's father who told him, as a boy, that he was "useless." Because of the husband's background, he might interpret careless statements from his wife as echoing the statements of his father. Because of the husband's background, he is extra sensitive in this area and thus more vulnerable to his wife's unloving words because deep inside his mind he is still clinging to a lie. So when the wife says to him impatiently, "You're supposed to have vacuumed the carpet, but you didn't sweep under the chairs!" he might hear her saying, "You're useless in helping me with the housework!"

Once the husband realizes, "Wait a second, I'm not useless," he is now positioned to make a choice. He can either absorb or reject the lie. In a best-case scenario, the husband will consciously decide to reject the lie. With that, he can decide to forgive his wife. He can think of the Lord's prayer: "And forgive us our debts as we forgive our debtors." The husband can also choose to "speak the truth in love" to his wife. Lovingly for the sake of building up his wife and sharpening her character, he can confront her. With sensitivity to the timing and wisdom in his approach he can let her know what she has done.

At that point, she then has to decide whether or not she will embrace the truth as well. Will she tell herself the truth? *What I've done has been damaging to my husband.* Will she be sorry for her husband's sake? *Lord, I'm so sorry; I don't want to hurt my husband.* Will she be humble enough to accept her husband's forgiveness? Or will she react in defensiveness and pride?

Both spouses are confronted with the opportunity to make wise choices. The husband has the opportunity to confront his wife instead of reacting with a counter-attack. The wife has the opportunity to receive a word of correction. Both spouses have a chance to practice wisdom. They can apply Scriptures such as Proverbs 25:11-12, "Like apples of gold in settings of silver is a word spoken in right circumstances. Like an earring of gold and an ornament of fine gold is a wise reprover to a listening ear" and Proverbs 9:8, "Reprove a wise [person] and [he/she] will love you."

By entering into godly sorrow. The final challenge is for the husband to encounter the living God in such a way that he feels godly sorrow—instead of the worldly sorrow that would cause him to keep blaming both his wife and his father and thus stay chained in bondage to his hot button.

Godly Sorrow and Worldly Sorrow

There's a difference between godly sorrow and worldly sorrow. Worldly sorrow is self-centered. It's a sorrow that regrets the consequences of a behavior that causes pain for the self. Worldly sorrow drives a person to want to be saved from their *situation,* not their sin. Worldly sorrow when caught in sin says, "I am sorry I got caught because then I wouldn't be in this mess! I am sad that I'm so hurt. I am sad for what I have lost. I am pained by how bad this makes me look. Dear God, please help me! I'm sorry because I know I broke your law, but now I need your help. I just want my life back. I just want to be happy."

Godly sorrow, by contrast, is God-centered. It grieves about sin before a holy God and embraces the truth about God's grace.

Godly sorrow breaks human pride. It brings about brokenness, causing a person to feel undone about their sin (Psalm 51:4; Isaiah 6:5). Godly sorrow is humble, and it leads to a repentance without regret (2 Corinthians 7:10). The difference between worldly sorrow and godly sorrow is summarized in table 8.1.

Table 8.1. The Difference Between Godly Sorrow and Worldly Sorrow

Godly Sorrow	Worldly Sorrow
Issue: Personal holiness	Issue: Personal Happiness
Begging for forgiveness	Begging for life enhancement
Broken by the reality of your sinfulness	Broken by the reality of your situation
Driven by humility	Driven by pride
Dignity and oneness restored	Depression and defensiveness remain
Compassion for who you hurt	Contempt toward who hurt you
Refreshed feeling	Drained feeling
Focused on truth	Focused on rationalizing your own sin
Focused on confession	Focused on circumstances
Justified by Christ	Justified by demands for your rights
Ownership of your sin	Victim of someone else's sin
Overwhelmed by gratitude to God	Overwhelmed by consequences of your sin
Produces abundant life	Produces death

| Sad for who you hurt | Sad for yourself |

Table 8.1

Coping with a Fallen World

People aren't born with hot buttons. We develop them after being hurt. Everyone has hot buttons because everyone has been sinned against by other people. It hurts to be sinned against; sometimes it's traumatic.

In marriage both spouses have the opportunity to help each other die to their old hot buttons. Some couples, however, practically make it a hobby to push each other's buttons instead of helping each other to heal.

Healing begins with compassion. For the first five years of our marriage, we had a vital shortage of compassion. Instead of softening our hearts and feeling empathy for each other we judged one another self-righteously. For example, I (Jim) was slow to assure Sarah about her looks. I never said anything negative; I never complained even once about her body. Occasionally I told her things such as, "Sarah, I never would have married you if I wasn't attracted to your whole body." But most of the time, I was resistant to assuring her in a way that convinced her of my love. What I communicated instead was that her problem was irrational and too vain to validate.

> **Everyone has hot buttons because everyone has been sinned against by other people.**

Conversely, I (Sarah) was slow to internalize that Jim genuinely was deceived about his intellect. I knew he had self-doubts, but it didn't soak in and register with me that, in given moments, he honestly believed that he was stupid. To me, it was obvious that he's smart. I saw it as self-indulgent for Jim to ask me to remind him of the positive affirmations he received from other people regarding his contributions and abilities.

See what we did to each other? We judged each other instead of ministering to each other. We dismissed each other's pain instead of *entering into* each other's pain. As a result, we missed the opportunity early in our marriage to help one another truly heal. A typical illustration of how our dynamics would play out is something like this.

I (Jim) would say something like, "Sarah, you have a funny look on your face."

Notice, Jim didn't tell me I (Sarah) was ugly. He made a comment about my countenance because he couldn't figure out what I was thinking. Had Jim emphasized before that he thinks my face is pretty, I might have kept perspective when he said that. But since I didn't *feel* pretty around him, I let my insecurity lead me to believe that Jim thought my face looked weird. What he *said* was, "Sarah, you have a funny look on your face." But what I *heard* was, "Sarah, you look odd instead of pretty." I reacted not to Jim but to my own interpretation of what Jim said. I reacted to the words I told myself.

A similar dynamic would happen if I would say to Jim something such as, "Of course, Honey, just think about it." What I was trying to communicate was "Jim, you're smart. Just use your able mind, and you'll get the concept." But what he heard was, "C'mon, Jim, get with the show. Everybody else understands."

Notice here again, Sarah didn't tell me (Jim) "to get with the show." She has never even hinted of that. But because of my past, I imagined the word *stupid* coming from her mouth. To me, it *felt* as though she said it because I echoed that message to myself. Consequently, I reacted to myself—to my own internal dialogue—while yet thinking my reaction was to Sarah.

It's interesting to note that our hot buttons don't match. I (Sarah) am not insecure about my intellect, and Jim's not insecure about his body. I'm no Einstein, and he's no Hercules, but if we're going to be honest, it's true that I have made a living with my intellect, and Jim has made a living with his looks. Part of our attraction to each other probably pertains to the refuge we have taken in each other.

At any rate, we're guilty for having reacted, and we're guilty for not having exercised love enough to have assured each other in our frailties. But we are changing that pattern. We're actually becoming nondefensive, and we're finding new joy in salving each other with compassion. We're also coaching one another to tell the truth to ourselves, so that we can let our hot buttons go.

Getting Psyched Out by Your Spouse

So much of building a marriage is building trust. Back in the days when Jim doubted that I (Sarah) thought he was smart, and I doubted that he found me attractive, we doubted one another's integrity. Even whenever I told Jim he was "witty," and even when he told me I "looked great," we suspected that the other one was just saying what we wanted to hear.

Trust between spouses must be cultivated; it doesn't just appear automatically. We've also built trust by hashing things out, sometimes splitting hairs, until each of us felt heard and accepted. But primarily our trust is based on the fact that we have forgiven one another.

Sometimes the level of a couple's mutual trust—or lack of trust—can be exposed in the strangest of ways. One night before we were married, we had a huge fight about whether or not boots are shoes. It's hard to explain how crazy and out-of-bounds that conversation went. At root, it had nothing to do with shoes and boots or even semantics. The issue we were fighting about was trust. How could Jim trust me if I would not admit that boots are *not* shoes? How could I trust Jim if he refused to believe that I have purchased boots at the *shoe* store?

Thankfully, we were able to talk to our good friend who had worked for over a decade in the shoe industry. He practically saved our engagement when he told us calmly and plainly that boots *and* shoes are both technically classified as "footwear." I (Sarah) can still hear Jim. "See?! I told you boots and shoes are not the same!" And I can still remember defending myself, "No, what our friend said is exactly what I've been saying all along! Boots are shoes, and shoes are shoes! Boots are footwear, and shoes are footwear!" And I can still remember Jim's retort, "Didn't you hear him? Boots are not shoes! They're footwear!"[2]

Not long ago at church, when I said something about Jim's and my fight regarding boots and shoes, an elder in our church started laughing. He said, "My wife and I can totally relate. For us it was pasta and spaghetti."

There are many ways to get psyched out by a spouse. An older friend of mine said one day she awakened, looked at her spouse of thirty-plus years, and wondered to herself, *Who is he?* She said it's possible to have an existential panic about your spouse, just as one might do when suddenly arrested by the disconcerting thought, *Who am I?* In a sense, *we don't know* exactly who we are because we're always in the process of changing—even at the cellular level. Our body cells are dying and being replaced, our personalities are being formed by every unfolding situation, and our relationship with our spouse is developing too—that's why the Bible says, "The two shall *become* one flesh." Accepting the reality of the dynamism of life—and not running away from it by jetting out of the marriage or jumping into an affair—is part of trusting God because our identity is hidden in him (Colossians 3:3).

Partners in Forgiveness

So far, we haven't panicked existentially about each other, but we can understand the disillusionment that comes when a spouse does something hurtful out of the ordinary that reminds you once again that they're not God. In God there is no shifting shadow (James 1:17). God is always true to his Word, always true to his nature, always true to himself. He can't even be tempted much less fail (James 1:13). Unlike the person you're married to, God has no latent tendency to be selfish. He has no painful childhood, no insecurities, no hot buttons. He never wakes up wondering who you are. He doesn't freak out if you say *shoes* instead of *boots* or *pasta* instead of *spaghetti.* It is wise to trust God because God is faithful.

Yet sometimes it's easy to start doubting God's character when issues in the marriage aren't resolved. It's tempting to blame God for marital hardship instead of taking responsibility for ourselves.

I (Jim) remember a time when I became angry at God for allowing me to get into our marriage. Sarah and I had been arguing, and I became so angry that I blew a fuse. For me, the ordeal climaxed into a gripping spiritual crisis. After storming out the door of our home, I yelled into the heavens, "This is an injustice! I'm stuck in this pit, this horrible marriage, for the rest of my life because of you, Lord! This is so unfair! If I wasn't a Christian, I could get a divorce. But now, because of my relationship with you, I have to live in misery the rest of my life. This is your fault, God!"

Then adding to my lament, I cried in desperation, "Change her, Lord!" and literally hurled my Bible in the air.

Suddenly I was seized by the fear of the Lord. What had I just done? Falling to my knees, I trembled in prayer, "Lord, I'm so sorry. Please, Lord, don't take your Spirit from me."

Wrenched by the reality of my wretchedness, my eyes were opened to the truth. It was *I* who needed to change. I felt overcome with grief at how I had treated Sarah and withheld my love from her. I also confessed my sin against God and repented from worldly sorrow.

I went home and told Sarah that I knew I needed to change. I told her the whole story about how gracious God had been and how sorry I had felt for brazenly accusing the Almighty. God was not at fault. I was.

Whatever we had been fighting about may have started with a hot button, but it ended in a rage. Yet God was right there with us. Because I had turned to God, and Sarah had turned to God while I was away, both of us had gained a fresh willingness to take ownership of our stuff.

Time and again we have gone to God, rediscovering our need for his forgiveness. In all our pettiness from past pain, immaturity from hot buttons, and sin from marital fights, we have found forgiveness in the Lord. Because God has forgiven us in Christ Jesus, we can forgive each other.

We are partners in forgiveness. That is how we managed our engagement, and that is how we live together now. Our relationship isn't easy, but it's strong—because forgiveness is the method that enables us to venture through this humbling life as one flesh.

9

BUILDING A CHRIST-CENTERED MARRIAGE

There are two main kinds of marriages in Western culture: contract marriages and covenant marriages. A *contract* marriage can loosely be defined as a legal agreement made by two people who bring certain expectations to the deal. In a contract marriage, each person agrees to put forth certain efforts for the other. A contract marriage is stipulation-based. It is built on conditional love. The contract endures only for as long as each person satisfactorily does their part. A contract marriage allows each spouse to say, "If you fail to meet my changing expectations and felt needs, I will punish you or call off the agreement."

A *covenant* marriage, by contrast, is rooted in a promise that two people make in the presence of God and other witnesses. In a covenant marriage each person vows to give their total being first to God and then to the other. A covenant marriage is relationship-based, not stipulation-based. The covenant endures because the promise is a permanent arrangement. A covenant marriage requires each spouse to say, "Even when you fail me, I will love you."

Marriage is meant to be a lifelong promise, not a temporal agreement, because marriage is designed to be a mirror of Christ's union with the church. Marriage is meant to be covenantal, not contractual.

What makes a marriage "Christian" is the couples' shared acknowledgment that Jesus Christ alone is Lord and Savior. What Jesus says is right, the couple says is right. What Jesus says is wrong, the couple says is wrong. As Jesus looked to Scripture, so a couple must look to Scripture. As Jesus turned to God, so a couple must turn to God. What makes a marriage "Christian" is that Christ is the center of the marriage.

Even in the church, it is rare for men and women to prioritize their relationship with Christ. When a couple falls in love, it is rare for them to consider whether their potential spouse helps them to love God more or not. Rare is the couple who truly makes Christ the center of their love relationship. When we teach marriage classes, I (Jim) always begin the first session by asking everyone there to say what it is that they appreciate most about their partner. Typically we hear answers such as

> "I like the way my partner listens to me."
> "I like how he makes me laugh."
> "I like it that she can throw a football."
> "I like how she challenges me to think."
> "I appreciate his ability to start things."
> "I appreciate that I feel loved."

Then we guide the group to consider how their partner contributes to their relationship with God. Sometimes the group is very responsive, and sometimes they're quiet because they've never stopped to think about that before.

To build a Christian marriage, both the husband and the wife must follow Christ. In our marriage, Jim has to want to be holy, and Sarah has to want to be holy. Otherwise, our claim to want to have a Christian marriage is only lip service. Holy matrimony begins with a holy desire to love the Lord God foremost (Matthew 22:36-38).

Honoring Christ Above All

Saying that Jesus comes first in our marriage is not to say we put "ministry" before marriage. We *are* each other's ministry! We have committed, as husband and wife, to minister Christ to one another. Yet more basic than our ministry to each other is our individual relationship with Christ. In other words, we are Christians first and a married couple second.

In the Old Testament book Song of Solomon, the groom calls his beloved, "my sister, my bride" (Song of Solomon 4:10). Similarly, I (Sarah) am Jim's wife, but more essentially than that, I am his sister in Christ. Jim is my husband, but more basically than that, he is my brother in Christ. All Christians are connected since we are comembers of Christ's body. In fact, all men and women are connected in the sense that all have been created by God. The basic principle of connectedness, as we mentioned before, is something Jesus taught to the Pharisees.

The Pharisees asked about the lawfulness of a Jewish man acquiring a divorce, but Jesus didn't answer on their terms. He talked about creation instead.

> Have you not read that He who created them from the beginning made them male and female, and said, "For this reason a man shall leave his father and mother and be joined to his wife, and the two shall become one flesh"? So they are no longer two, but one flesh. What therefore God has joined together, let no man separate. (Matthew 19:4-6)

It's because God "made them male and female" that a man shall "be joined to his wife." Man and woman are designed to be together, even in an unmarried state. It is not coincidental that the very first words that Adam said to Eve were words that celebrated their oneness—even though they were still single. Adam said, "This is now bone of my bones, and flesh of my flesh; She shall be called Woman [not Wife], because she was taken out of Man" (Genesis 2:23).

This insight from Genesis brings perspective to the fact that the woman was created "for" the man. In 1 Corinthians 11:9, Paul says, "For indeed man was not created for the woman's sake, but woman for the man's sake." Typically it's the wife who is told to cleave to her husband as if cleaving were synonymous to submitting. And following this passage, one might expect the commandment to cleave to have been issued to the woman, not the man. Since the woman was created "for" the man, it would seem as though the Bible would say, "For this reason a *woman* should be joined to her husband since she was created *from* him and *for* him."

But God gave the commandment to the man. God commands the *husband* to leave, and *him* to cleave to the one who was created for him. According to the Bible—in both the Old Testament and the New Testament, and even from the mouth of Jesus—the man is responsible to cleave (Genesis 2:24; Matthew 19:6; Ephesians 5:31).

The husband, as head, is told to cleave to his wife, not divorce her. He is instructed to leave his *parents,* not his wife. In essence, he's commanded to leave his parents' expectations and obey God's commandments instead. Thus marriage gives a couple a fresh opportunity to establish Christian patterns in a family.

One of the worship leaders at our church, Charlie, shared his testimony of having grown up in a non-Christian family. For him, being a Christian has been difficult because he's the only believer in his family. During holidays he's been mocked by other members of his family for believing in the miracle of the virgin birth. For years Charlie was single and thus subjected to his family's angry taunts. But now, in a sense, he has "left" his family because he's cleaving to Griselda, his new wife, and establishing with her a new family pattern of worshiping Christ during holidays.

God Comes First

Without exception, every single time that we have sinned against each other, we have first sinned against God. We turn away from God *before* we turn away from each other. Our posture toward God necessarily informs the way we conduct ourselves in marriage.

I (Sarah) cannot communicate how positive the impact is on our marriage when Jim is refreshed in the Lord. When he takes time away to listen to God in solitude, invariably he becomes a better husband. Every time he gains a fresh awareness of God's grace, he becomes less defensive, slower to blame, and more patient and kind. My favorite thing, in fact, is for Jim to preach a good sermon because as soon as he finishes, he forgets that he's embarrassed to be affectionate in public. Suddenly he becomes this unselfconscious husband whose heart is overflowing with gratitude and love. He apologizes for things that I well may have forgotten about. He clutches me and kisses me right there in the front row! When we get home from church, he feels so good before God that he literally tends to carry me around the house.

Similarly, I'm a better wife when I let down my guard before the Lord. Instead of being caught up in myself, I can put my focus on Jim. I can empathize with his struggles and see his point of view more clearly. I can generate more energy to communicate how important he is to me. When I bring myself to God, I also can pray more humble prayers. For instance, I can pray for Jim to be healed from the wounds that have been caused by my sharp tongue. I can pray for him to be hopeful. I can pray for him to experience God's comfort. When finally I become nondefensive, I can minister to Jim instead of vainly looking out for myself.

We're fooling ourselves if we say "our marriage" is a problem in and of itself. There is no such entity as "the marriage of Jim and Sarah Sumner" apart from the two of us personally. To put it more simply, we are our marriage. Our marriage is us. Whenever we have a problem, both of us are responsible to own that problem—because that problem is ours. Jim's and my marriage is what we make of it. Our relationship with each other flows from our relationship with God.

Since how we live together is defined by who we are, we are striving to live "above the line" in our character as individuals and jointly in our marriage as one. To live above the line means to emulate Christ by doing the right thing in the right way at the right time.

There's a tool for helping people to do this. I (Sarah) call it the People Model, a framework loosely based on Plato's philosophical ideals of the true, the good and the beautiful. The People Model was born from a premise that people tend to operate in accordance with their personal values. Each of us adheres to a set of motivations that drives the way we relate to other people. The values we hold can dramatically clash, but these *seemingly* clashing values actually fit together beautifully as long as they are kept above the line. There's an ethical dimension to the People Model because in all three categories, a person can either be "above the line" (doing what's right) or "below the line" (doing what's wrong). The goal of the model is help people rise above the line *in all three categories.*

After I recently presented the People Model to a crowd of college students, it was the *married ministry leaders* who beelined to me first. Intuitively they could see that the People Model applies to every marriage. In my book *Leadership Above the Line* I spell out in more detail how the People Model works.[1] Here in this chapter, we will only offer an abbreviated glimpse of how it works. Our purpose in doing so is to resource Christian couples with a vision of what it means to develop an above-the-line marriage.

The People Model

There are essentially three types of people: Strategists, Humanitarians and Diplomats. While most people lean primarily toward one type, everyone is a *mix* of all three types. To put it very succinctly, Strategists tend to value clarity, accountability and integrity. Humanitarians tend to value loyalty, patience and compassion. Diplomats tend to value a sense of unity, refinement and peace. (See figure 9.1.)

STRATEGISTS	HUMANITARIANS	DIPLOMATS
Clarity	Loyalty	Sense of Unity
Accountability	Patience	Refinement
Integrity	Compassion	Peace

Figure 9.1. Values of three types of people.

Generally speaking, Strategists want the facts out on the table so they can get problems resolved. Humanitarians, by contrast, are sensitive to people's feelings. Because Humanitarians tend to be mindful of the human factor, they typically find the strength to forbear hard situations when problems are not ready to be solved. Diplomats, by contrast, focus more intuitively on the timing and the mood of a given situation because Diplomats deal with problems indirectly. They like to figure out ways to finesse them. (See figure 9.2.)

STRATEGISTS	HUMANITARIANS	DIPLOMATS
Clarity	Loyalty	Sense of Unity
Accountability	Patience	Refinement
Integrity	Compassion	Peace
Facts	Feelings	Timing/Mood
Fix the problem	Forbear the problem	Finesse the problem

Figure 9.2. How the values of three types of people play out when problems arise.

Jesus was a first-rate Strategist, a first-rate Humanitarian and a first-rate Diplomat. As an above-the-line Strategist, he spoke clearly when he confronted Peter, "Get behind Me, Satan!" after Peter tried to sway him away from being willing to be killed (Matthew 16:22-23). Jesus also held people accountable. On the night before he died, he kept awakening his disciples in the Garden of Gethsemane, telling them to pray instead of sleep (Matthew 26:40-45). He also was a man of integrity who never forgot who he was

(Matthew 16:13-17). He didn't shy away from the disheartening truth that Judas was going to betray him (John 6:59-71). He was bold to clear the temple when the Lord's house of prayer became a raucous marketplace of corruption (John 2:13-17).

As an above-the-line Humanitarian, Jesus was loyal to his disciples even when they doubted him (Matthew 28:16-20). He was patient with Simon the Pharisee who was arrogant and unkind to the woman (the "sinner") who washed Jesus' feet with her tears (Luke 7:36-50). He was compassionate to the multitudes, unlike the disciples who wanted to send them away (Luke 9:12-17). He was so gentle that as soon as he and his disciples found out that John the Baptist had been murdered, Jesus told his disciples to rest (Mark 6:21-32). In addition to that, Jesus was remarkably forbearing, calling Judas "Friend" even on the night he betrayed him (Matthew 26:50).

As a Diplomat, Jesus valued unity to the point of making it the theme of his last prayer in the Garden of Gethsemane (John 17:20-26). Jesus understood that when unity is perfected, it's perceived—because when people are fully unified, they know it. Thus Jesus told his disciples to express their unity by loving one another so that the world might also perceive their Christianity (John 13:35). Jesus also had a brilliant way with words. He could attract huge throngs of people with his teachings. He was also the greatest peacemaker in the world. The apostle Paul said Jesus "is" our peace (Ephesians 2:14). Moreover, his sense of timing was impeccable. He waited in silence before opening his mouth and speaking unrestrainedly to Pilate (John 19:8-12). It's inspiring to imagine how much impact Jesus' well-timed words must have had. And when the Pharisees tried to trap him by asking impossible questions, Jesus always found a way to finesse the situation and put the pressure back on them.

Jesus stayed above the line as he lived out his values. The rest of us occasionally fall below the line. (See figure 9.3.)

STRATEGISTS	HUMANITARIANS	DIPLOMATS
Clarity	*Loyalty*	*Unity*
Accountability	*Patience*	*Refinement*
Integrity	*Compassion*	*Promoting a Sense of Peace*
Facts	*Feelings*	*Timing / Mood*
Fix the problem	*Forbear the problem*	*Finesse the problem*
Self-righteous	*Self-serving*	*Self-absorbed*
Harsh Judgment	*People-pleasing*	*Image Management*
Presumptuous/Prideful	*Guilty/Afraid*	*Deceitful/Manufacturing Spin*

Figure 9.3. "Below the line" behaviors

When Strategists fall below the line, they become self-righteous. They become overzealous in their quest to champion truth and integrity. Thus they can tend to be harsh. Below-the-line Strategists tend to be impatient, prideful, and presumptuous. They often feel convinced that they know best, even before they listen to all the facts.

When Humanitarians fall below the line, they become self-serving by getting tangled up in people-pleasing. Their care for other people crumbles and corrodes into a fear of displeasing people. Below-the-line Humanitarians feel guilty for holding on to their own perspective. Consequently, they devote their best energy to appeasing other people instead of helping other people to identify and repent from root problems.

When Diplomats fall below the line, they become self-absorbed. They fall into the trap of image management. Selfishly they use their refinement and charisma as a means of manipulating people. Below-the-line Diplomats are deceitful. They take advantage of other people by convincing other people of their spin.

The People Model in Marriage

Awareness of these tendencies in people can make a positive difference in a marriage. For example, what if two Strategists are married and both of them fall below the line? What is likely to happen? They're going to fight. They'll war with each other because both will be convinced that they are right. Both of them will talk instead of listen. Both will be critical and harsh. Both will be self-righteously judgmental. Both will be heavily biased against the other. Moreover, both will be quick to blame the other one instead of protecting the other person with understanding.

But if both Strategists are humble enough to rise above the line, they will be set up to enjoy a solid marriage that is purified by forgiveness and strengthened by the power of accountability. They will thrive by being honest. They will also learn firsthand, on the basis of their trust, what it means to experience great freedom. They will heartily welcome input that's insightful and corrective because correction breeds integrity, and integrity is what Strategists are about.

What if two Humanitarians are married? What's probably going to happen when they fall below the line? They will avoid conflict like the plague. As a result, sooner or later they'll harbor bitterness while yet rationalizing to themselves that they don't want to hurt the other one's feelings. They'll feel guilty about things that they did—and did not—do. They'll feel too scared to uphold high standards. Not only will they continue to put up with bad behavior from their spouse, but they'll also prefer to be enabled in their own sin too.

If both Humanitarians exercise the courage to rise above the line, not only will be they feel supported and accepted, but they'll also be encouraged to grow. They will grant each other space to make mistakes. They'll be sensitive and attentive to each other's stress. They'll empathize with each other's feelings. Overall, their marriage will be comfortable and warm. Their marriage will run smoothly because it will be bathed in compassion.

Two Diplomats who fall below the line together could easily pretend that their marriage is far better than it is. The two of them could excel in convincing other people that their problems are too minimal to mention. They could tacitly agree to channel their best energy into making themselves look innocent and holy. Yet privately they could wage a marital war. They could even make a game out of smiling at each other in public while yet stabbing one another in the back.

On the flip side, if both Diplomats are honest enough to rise above the line, they truly could have a model marriage. They could laugh at themselves instead of taking themselves too seriously. They could honor the canons of wise timing and not panic when a problem showed up. They could prioritize their unity, taking pains to understand each other's perceptions. As Diplomats, they could deal with conflicts more successfully by prefacing their remarks with helpful caveats instead of being too blunt or too avoidant.

What about marriages that are mixed? If a Strategist were married to a Diplomat, and both were to fall below the line, there would probably be an automatic tension between the two because the Strategist wouldn't stand for the Diplomat's dishonesty, and the Diplomat wouldn't stand for the divisiveness of the Strategist's pride. But if both were to rise above the line, they could be a super dynamic duo. The Strategist could help the Diplomat be authentic instead of political. The Diplomat could help the Strategist to implement wise timing. Moreover, the Strategist could help the Diplomat to prioritize integrity while the Diplomat helped the Strategist to see that unity is an aspect of integrity.

If a Diplomat were married to a Humanitarian, and both were to fall below the line, the Diplomat would most likely take advantage of the Humanitarian. For example, if a Humanitarian spouse were to suggest the couple go to marriage counseling, the Diplomat spouse might attempt to manipulate the perceptions of the counselor favorably toward the Diplomat. The Humanitarian might resent that but feel too scared to do anything much about it except talk behind the Diplomat's back. Cleverly the Diplomat might decide at that point, to confess just enough to satisfy the counselor and stir the Humanitarian's sense of sympathy. The Diplomat then seizes the opportunity to start the whole cycle again. Thus the Humanitarian still continues to get used, and thus the Christian couple stays stuck.

But if the Diplomat and Humanitarian both were to rise above the line, they could merge their different strengths to build each other's character beautifully. The Humanitarian could help the Diplomat to value people personally instead of using them for personal advantage. The Diplomat could help the Humanitarian to detach emotionally instead of personalizing things too much. Each could help the other with personal boundaries. The Humanitarian could help the Diplomat not to detach away in self-absorption, and the Diplomat could help the Humanitarian to relax enough to laugh instead sinking into self-consciousness and anxiety.

If a Strategist were married to a Humanitarian, and both of them were to fall below the line, the Strategist would likely be impatient, judging the Humanitarian as "touchy-feely," while the Humanitarian would be inclined to spoil the Strategist by being codependent and enduring the Strategist's pride. Over time, the Humanitarian would be wearied and probably spring a root of bitterness in reaction. The Strategist, at that point—instead of repenting—would probably scold the Humanitarian for holding a grudge.

If, however, both the Strategist and Humanitarian were to rise above the line, they could live as iron sharpening iron. The Strategist could sharpen the

Humanitarian by helping the Humanitarian value truth, even when the truth caused discomfort. The Humanitarian, by contrast, could sharpen the Strategist by helping the Strategist to empathize with people instead of trying so hard to fix them. The Strategist, moreover, could sharpen the Humanitarian by helping the Humanitarian to take responsibility for his (or her) emotions instead of being haunted by guilt. The Humanitarian, in turn, could help the Strategist to believe that mercy truly triumphs over judgment.

Imitating Christ

Love is the key to rising and remaining above the line. If every Christian couple were to imitate Christ and honor him as the center of their marriage, they would be set up to have a great marriage regardless of their personality types. If people really want to be like Jesus, they *must* make it their goal to rise above the line *in all three* categories—because Jesus lived his life above the line in all three categories.

Apart from love, a person might only *seem* to be above the line. The apostle Paul put it this way—more or less—in 1 Corinthians 13:1-3:

> If I speak with the tongues of a great Diplomat and can dazzle a crowd with my extraordinary sense of propriety and refinement and can unify people for the purpose of world peace, yet I don't have love, I have become a noisy gong or clanging cymbal. And if I am a great Strategist who can shed light on situations and analyze the facts, and mastermind plans and live honestly and boldly in integrity, but I don't love, then I am nothing. And if I serve self-sacrificially as a great Humanitarian who loyally extends patience and compassion and serves people to the point of delivering my body to burned, but don't love, it profits me nothing.

Without love, the Strategist is self-righteous, the Humanitarian self-serving, and the Diplomat self-absorbed. But by the power of the

Holy Spirit, it's possible for a person to make progress. Married couples can make progress as well. Rising above the line is like becoming one flesh in that neither happens instantaneously. It takes time to develop Christian character. It takes time to be transformed. Over time, married couples can become one flesh in their back-and-forth ways of communicating together, making joint decisions and emulating Christ by living above the line in all three categories.

10

EVERY COUPLE'S NEED FOR CHRISTIAN COMMUNITY

During the first year of our marriage, we used to meet with another Christian couple every Friday night. One evening when we were telling them about a problem in our marriage, we started fighting right in front of them. I (Sarah) was being highly sarcastic, while Jim was being bull-headed, pushing all the blame on me. I could talk faster, but Jim could talk more loudly. The more I talked, the louder he became. The louder he became, the more I talked.

The husband, Patrick, interrupted us. He looked at me and said matter-of-factly, "Jim just doesn't get it."

I could hardly believe my ears. Both Patrick and his wife Kelly saw what I saw. Both of them were convinced that Jim was blinded by his pride. I knew I liked that couple. I was totally delighted we were there. Right about then, Patrick leaned into the table around which we were all sitting, jutted out his chin and looked directly and imposingly at me. Contorting his countenance, he craned his neck and turned his head toward mine. Hovering just inches away, he wagged his chin dramatically right in front of my face. There was no way I could miss it when he emphatically announced with clear enunciation, "And Sarah, what you're doing would drive me crazy!"

Jim was ready to give him a high-five. Yet that double confrontation made a lifelong impact on us. Both of us were jolted into paying more attention to what we each needed to change. It helped us to be validated, and it helped to be confronted so plainly.

We could probably recount a hundred more stories of how we have been helped by other members of

Christ's body. People in the church have been there for us. We've never been alone in times of need. People have shown up to serve as witnesses on our behalf whenever we've needed them for a Matthew 7 and 18 conversation. They've been there when we needed them to pray. They've been there for us—and endured us—right in the thick of our junk. They've watched us fight. They've seen our immaturity in action.

But they've also witnessed our growth. They've even helped us celebrate our growth. Our close friend, Patricia Lentz, who was listening to us talk one Saturday morning and said, "You guys need to hover. In the last two hours, you have just resolved nine or ten different issues. You have had an amazing conversation. You two can connect in so many detailed ways. I think you need to hover. Take a pause for the rest of the day because you guys have a lot to celebrate." Being in Christian community not only helps us grow and change; it also helps us celebrate our growth.

Still Pressing On

We are in our twelfth year of marriage, and just a few months ago, I (Sarah) asked our friends, Ray and Janice from church, to have lunch with us so that I could confess my anxiety about having lapsed back into the trap of reacting to Jim in sarcasm. Jim, likewise, had crept back toward the edge of becoming fatalistic again.

Janice looked at us and said, "Have you had any training in conflict resolution? Have you been taught how to use 'I language' and not 'you language?' To speak in first person, so that you start your sentences 'I' instead of 'you'?"

She went on. "I sometimes have to say to Ray, 'I feel insecure, and I hate it when I feel insecure, so now I'm mad!'" Her comment was so disarming that we both loosened up. We couldn't help but chuckle. Yes, we had been trained to use those skills. We've even taught those skills to others. It's just that we forget to use those skills. We had been hurling "you statements" at each other:

"You and your expectations!"

"You don't even realize what you do!"

We would mingle in apologies and try to forgive each other, but then a few days later, the cycle would start up again because we were not addressing the real issues.

It was unbelievably timely when Janice then interjected, "Have you ever cried together in your efforts to communicate? Have you ever been that vulnerable together before? Ray and I have spoken to each other through agonizing tears, so strenuous have been our efforts to try to hear what the other one is saying."

Ray added, "We *want* to understand one another, but sometimes we can't. Even after thirty years of marriage! It's still hard sometimes."

We were silenced by their instruction. Silenced and inspired. We knew we hadn't done that recently. We knew we hadn't done that. We knew we hadn't tried that intently to listen and hear each other.

By the power of Christian community—the body of Christ at

work—we left that lunch feeling renewed. We also left with greater sensitivity. I (Jim) realized I had squelched Sarah's attempts to tell me what she needed and how she felt. And Sarah saw with greater clarity that she was bypassing the process of communicating vulnerably with Jim because she was afraid of being invalidated again.

Our problems are so solvable. They're recurrent, yes, but thanks in part to the help of our Christian friends, they're diminishing. Just recently I (Sarah) had lunch with our prayer-warrior friend Becky, who's been married for almost thirty-four years. At one point in our conversation, she said point-blank, "It took Don and me twenty years to work through our major problems."

I laughed heartily. It was a painful laugh, as if my funny bone had been hit. It hurt to hear the truth about their marriage, yet the truth was very comforting because it normalized Jim's and my experience.

Becky smiled triumphantly. "But we did it," she said. "We've come through it now. We've been through it for over a decade."

Holy Incompatibility

Every Christian couple needs to be in Christian community. Couples who get along well need it every bit as much as couples who argue and fight. Being active in Christ's body is part of what it means to love the church's head, Christ Jesus.

Authentic Christian community is interpersonal. Being in it is not the same as merely attending church. In fact, it's possible—even common—for Christians to go to church without ever participating in authentic fellowship with other believers. To be in Christian community is to be *relationally connected* with other people who are connected to Christ, the head.

Apart from Christian community, couples are prone either to fall into a pit of marital fights or into a den of artificial marital oneness, a false sense of oneness that couples experience when cooperating together in sin. For us the main temptation has usually been to fight. We try so hard not to sin together that we end up sinning by fighting.

Some married couples never have bad fights. It all just depends on the couple's temperaments, their levels of maturity, and what their personal histories entail. A lot of it also depends on how compatible two people are, especially with regard to their style of sinning. Whenever I (Sarah) lecture to undergraduate students, frequently I exhort them to marry someone whose sins are incompatible with their own.

"Marry a person who isn't entertained by your sin," I say. "Marry someone who isn't fun to be with whenever you're indulging in your favorite way of being unlike Christ. Marry someone who likes you best when you're following God, and likes you least when you're not. Otherwise, it will be too easy to fall into the trap of conspiring in sin with the person you want to marry while yet telling yourself that 'we're so good for each other.'"

How many Christian couples regularly experience a false sense of oneness by joining together in sin? How often do Christian couples happily indulge in bad patterns of togetherness without holding one another accountable? How many Christian couples don't even think twice about gossiping together, being lazy together, overeating together, overspending together, drowning in debt together, laughing at coarse humor together, being prayerless together, being worldly together, and on and on?

Imagine what would happen if partners in a marriage were sarcastic, for example. It's not unreasonable to expect that they would congratulate themselves whenever they came up with "a good one." They might be sarcastic against other people, perhaps by cutting down political figures or someone they disdain in the media. Or they might be sarcastic in their fights against each other. Or they might be sarcastic when angry at themselves about something. In any of these cases, the chances are very high that the couple would deny the reality of what sarcasm does.

Growing up, my brother and I (Sarah) denied the destructiveness of sarcasm, especially since we used it primarily against ourselves. For years we engaged in a pattern of canceling out each other's ridiculous overstatements by carrying them to the point of absurdity. For instance, if one of us said something outlandish such as, "I'm the worst Christian in the world," the other one might retort, "Well, actually, you're the very worst Christian in history." Then we'd laugh and be sympathetic with each other's feelings because we understood that one of us was venting. To us, sarcasm was a game.

Jim doesn't see it as a game. Jim rightly sees it as a weapon. Time and again he has argued a strong case against the arrogance and unseemliness of sarcasm. More than a few times he's confronted me about it in the presence of other believers. Though I've always apologized after doing it, for a long time in our marriage I didn't have godly sorrow. I was sorry on the surface, but underneath the surface, I was flippant.

The problem eventually culminated one night when it was raining, and we were driving in southwest Texas in the country on a back road. Jim and I were having a conflict about something, and both of us let the argument get too heated. I remember the pounding rain, the darkness and the limited visibility. And I remember being angry, venting my frustrations, trying to get Jim to see where he was wrong, and indulging myself by hurling sarcastic remarks. Out came a burst that I will never forget. Jim raged, almost yelping.

"You're ripping me apart!" he cried.

The depth of his cry left me shuddered. Nothing more was said for over an hour. The rain outside kept beating on our vehicle, forbidding me to forget what I had done.

Until that stormy night, I had minimized the truth about my incisive tongue. I had claimed that I wasn't all that guilty because my words were not frontal attacks. I have never called Jim names or anything like that. What I've tended to do instead is echo what I've heard him saying to me: "Oh, I'm sure the problem is entirely my fault! It couldn't have a thing to do with you! You're probably the most loving husband in the country! Anyone with any drop of sanity, no doubt, would side with you!" Knowing that my statements were inverted like this, I rationalized that my sarcasm wasn't terrible.

But then I heard that yelping cry. It was a cry of anguish, and because it came from Jim, it haunted me.

Providentially a few weeks later, I ran across the word *sarcasm* and decided to take a look at it in Greek. I had known this before but forgotten: the word *sarcasm* derives from the Greek word *sarx* meaning "flesh." The Greek word *sarkazein* literally means "to rend the flesh." No wonder I was halted by Jim's yelp in the car that night. My husband's flesh had been ripped—by me.

The Danger of Self-Defense

It's much, much easier to break destructive patterns in the context of community with other members of the body of Christ. Both of us have experienced a number of spiritual breakthroughs by being willing to admit our failures. If Jim hadn't exercised the process of Matthew 18 by years ago telling our friends about my sarcasm, I may not have been receptive to the conviction of the Spirit in the car the night Jim told me I was ripping him apart. I also may not have chosen to arrange to confess to Ray and Janice at lunch. Thanks to Jim and others in Christ's body, I am less deaf than before. Thanks to them, I understand better how violent sarcasm really is. Though I still quench the Holy Spirit when I'm caught up in self-defense, my heart is a little softer than before.

Another experience helped me (Sarah) even further. Not surprisingly, it also happened in a context of community. One night one of the wives in our small group of married couples said she felt "steamrolled" by her husband. She said she couldn't help but withdraw from her husband because he constantly trampled over her.

Almost instantly the husband reacted. "Steamrolled?!" he said, as if insulted. "I don't steamroll you! That's not fair to say!"

Jim tried to calm the husband. "Look, I know you don't really steamroll her. Women don't understand what *steamroll* means to a man. You have the power to steamroll her if you wanted to, but that's completely different from what you've done."

The wife reasserted her complaint. "I'm saying that I *feel* like you steamroll me."

Again the husband reacted. That's when the realization suddenly hit me. I said to the husband, "You're just trying to defend yourself, right? Your words aren't meant to be *offensive against her;* they're meant to be defensive on behalf of yourself."

"Exactly!" he exclaimed. "That's exactly what it is. I'm just trying to protect myself."

I stood up on my feet and said to the husband, "I understand your intention, but it's precisely your self-defense—all the words you say when you're trying to protect yourself—that are hurting your wife and tempting her to pull away from you. Your wife feels as if she's being steamrolled by you right when you're defending yourself."

It was a huge moment in our small group. Not only did the husband learn something about himself that he wasn't able to hear from his wife, but his wife learned something too. She came to understand that her husband had the impression that she withdrew herself intentionally for the purpose of punishing him. He saw *her withdrawal* as an offense. By contrast, she saw her withdrawal as an act of self-defense. From the wife's perspective, she was sheltering herself from an overpowering husband.

I learned something too. I realized that my sarcasm, though intended as self-*defense,* came to Jim as a counter*offense.* Understanding this has enabled me to see that my past excuses of "just echoing Jim in his claims of being right" are not as harmless or legitimate as I once thought. My sarcastic defenses are aggressive offenses against my husband.

This particular dynamic is a common one in marriage. One spouse thinks that in kicking away the other, they're merely looking out for themselves. But when they themselves get kicked by the other, they interpret the same action as a deliberate offense maliciously devised against them.

The Love-Trap of Money

Perhaps the most popular sin of all for Christian couples to indulge in, at least in America, is greed. Statistics verify that the problem is pervasive. Debt levels are very similar between Christians and nonChristians. Giving levels are similar as well. Only about 3 percent of Christians in America give even close to a tithe of their income, 57 percent give something once in a while, and 40 percent don't give anything at all to further the cause of our head, Jesus Christ.

If every American Christian tithed a straight 10 percent of their income, the church would accrue $143 billion. Reports from the United Nations project that it would take only $70-80 billion to meet the health care and educational needs of the entire population of poor people in the world. The church *singlehandedly* could take care of the world's poor with $60-70 billion left over for evangelistic efforts.

These statistics aren't new. Most of us have heard them, or something similar to them, more than once. Why do we remain unmoved? Why do Christian couples tend to hold so tightly to their money? Why don't Christian couples decide to give more?

Most Christians practice *transactional* giving patterns. A person gives financially from an inner motivation of guilt, duty or pride. Transactional giving usually occurs sporadically. It's mechanical, not spiritual. Often it is triggered externally.

Christianity, however, is not about transactions. Christianity is about transformation. Transformational giving flows from a person's inner being. It's internally motivated, and it's joyful. Martin Luther once suggested that there are three levels of conversion in a Christian: the head, the heart and the wallet. Conversion of the wallet nearly always comes last. Most Christian couples will continue to be trapped by the worldly love of money until they finally decide *to be open about their finances* in trusted Christian community with other believers.

Who can deny that Christians in America generally believe that money is an entirely private matter? In men's small groups, I (Jim) have found that it's easier to get men to talk about sex than money. Even family members are reticent to be open with one another about their financial decisions. In truth, how people spend their money tells a lot about their hearts—what they value, what they believe in, and what they prioritize.

I once asked our congregation to close their eyes and imagine they had just won $25,000 on a game show, and that all of it in cash was handed to them personally in a briefcase filled with stacks of $100 bills. "What thoughts and images come to mind?" I said. "Did anyone visualize themselves holding up the money in the air, giving thanks to God, praying that you'd use it for his glory? Or did you find yourself imagining how you would spend the money on yourself?" In the book of 1 Timothy, the apostle Paul urges Timothy to "flee" from the love of money and pursue godliness instead (1 Timothy 6:11). Many Christian couples honestly believe they really don't have a problem "loving money." Yet their spending habits—and their unwillingness to talk openly about their spending habits—indicate otherwise.

Let's face it, Christians are susceptible to internalizing the message that we are constantly bombarded with: *Earn more, so you can get what you want.* Apart from Christian community, we will rarely hear the message: *Give more, so you can supply what is needed.* If we really don't love money, and we really do love God foremost, then it seems that we'd be eager to open our lives in trusted community with each other, even to the point of discussing how we're handling our money. It seems that we'd also be eager to teach our children by way our own example. Why is it so rare for Christians to band together and help one another cultivate generous hearts?

Sharing openly in Christian community about financial matters has nothing to do with legalism. Legalism drives *transactional* giving. Though someone might argue that it's wrong to discuss finances in Christian community because our giving is supposed to be "in secret," it's pretty safe to say that the Pharisees whom Jesus rebuked for displaying their spiritual almsgiving were not giving sacrificially. The Pharisees weren't thinking about God and the people God loves who need help. They were thinking about themselves.

Unlike legalism, which is coercive, *transformational* giving is unconstrained. Transformational giving comes from a heart that knows that "love of money" is a trap. For any Christian couple to ask for accountability is for them to freely choose to be prodded toward greater godliness. When we talk to fellow Christians about our finances, we're not inviting them to snoop into our bank account or pressure us to mimic their convictions. We're asking them to bear witness to the condition of our hearts.

How can any couple profess to be following Jesus without heeding Jesus' teachings on money? Jesus talked *more* about the proper use of money than he did about prayer or sexual purity or keeping the law. Jesus made it clear that it's impossible to love God and love money all at once. "No one can serve two masters; for either he will hate the one and love the other, or he will be devoted to one and despise the other. You cannot serve God and wealth" (Matthew 6:24). The writer of Hebrews said something similar:

> Make sure that your character is free from the love of money, being content with what you have; for He Himself has said, "I will never desert you, nor will I ever forsake you," so that we confidently say, "The Lord is my Helper, I will not be afraid. What will man do to me?" Remember those who led you, who spoke the word of God to you; and considering the result of their conduct, imitate their faith. (Hebrews 13:5-7)

How can we imitate each other's faith with regard to our giving habits unless we open up our lives to each other? We *want* fellow believers to see who we are. We don't want to live in secret. We're not trustworthy enough to live apart from Christ's body.

When we were first married, Sarah had been a Christian for thirty years, and I had been a Christian for two years. Whereas she had cultivated a generous heart, I found much of my security and identity in our money. To Sarah it was unthinkable for us *not* to be generous with our finances. She insisted we give at least 10 percent of our monthly income to God's work. Her desire was to give even more.

When we moved to California in 1997, our combined net income was $2300 a month. So writing a monthly check of $250 was a discipline for me. How were we going to make it doing that? And what were we giving up? It's not hard to do the math. We could've taken a nice vacation or in three years time bought a new car or something. So I suggested to Sarah that we give only 3 percent. But she saw that as a lack of generosity and a lack of trust in God. What if Sarah had been like me? If my wife was just like me, we'd still be giving no more than 3 percent.

My (Sarah's) own personal journey of becoming a giver has everything to do with being connected to other members of Christ's body. Apart from people at church, I never would have given *sacrificially.*It's the Christian community who influenced my heart. I don't want to sit on my rocking chair when I'm old, knowing that God gave me multiple opportunities to make a big tangible difference in other people's lives—and yet I didn't give to them because I wanted to spend my money either on myself or my kids. To me, that's a nightmare. I want to be able to identify with those who can sit around telling stories about the sacrificial giving goals they met over the years—like Greg and Julie Nettle, our friends at Rivertree Christian Church in Ohio. When I heard their story, I said, "That's it. I just know God is calling Jim and me to do something similar."

After weeks of praying about how much they should give, Greg and Julie set a goal to give $78,000 in one year strictly to the work of Christian ministry. At the time they pledged it, their combined income was about $200,000 a year. When a few months later it became evident that they were not going to be able to start a family unless Julie could quit her job, together they decided she should quit. That major change dropped their annual income to $75,000. Being people of integrity, they went to the church board and asked if they could be released from their pledge. Although they'd only given $25,000 so far, the board graciously granted their request.

But when Greg and Julie prayed again to God, they didn't hear God telling them it was okay to renege. In fact, they heard just the opposite. But how were they going to muster up $53,000? Most of their money was tied up in their house. The only other financial asset they even had was a bank account Greg's mother had encouraged him to start back when he was fourteen. As a discipline, Greg had contributed $20 or more to it monthly—for years—letting compound interest do its work.

Guess how much cash had accumulated over the years? Right about $53,000. To Greg and Julie, this was a clear sign from God. They gave every dime of it to fulfill the rest of their pledge.

To this day, Greg and Julie testify that they've never felt more joy. The freedom, the excitement, the assurance that *together they had trusted the living*

God lifted their spirit in such a way that nothing else has ever had the power to do.

There's now a marvelous movement of the Holy Spirit in Rivertree Christian Church. Not only are Greg and Julie sacrificial givers, their whole church is focused very particularly on giving to orphans. In 2006 alone, Rivertree, a community of a little less than three thousand people, gave $290,000 to Compassion International, a Christian organization that ministers spiritually and financially to needy children. That same year, Rivertree's regular giving, aside from their gift to Compassion, went up by 35 percent from the prior year. Now their local church can also give generously—in the name of Christ, our head—to people in their local community.

How many Christian couples would *stop fighting* about money if together they'd start setting giving goals? How many would start fighting if they'd hold one another accountable for overspending? How many children would grow up to be lifelong givers if parents would model what it means to have a joyful generous heart? How many hurting people would be helped if the body of Christ would love them to the point of giving sacrificially?

Chances are very high that until Christian couples get involved in Christian community to the point of talking openly about their finances—and their marriages—most will stay stuck in the patterns that they're currently trapped in.

The Benefit of Christian Community

Christian couples aren't supposed to stay trapped in any sin. Though all of us stumble in many ways, we can all keep growing and changing. In Christ we don't have to stay stuck. By the strength of Christian community, the full body of Christ—which extends worldwide—Christian couples can truly become transformed people. Whether a couple is trapped in materialism and money, bickering and bitterness, addictions and enablement, or sexual infidelity of any kind, there is hope.

Hope prevails for those who choose to walk in the light of truth. There is hope for any couple who honestly wants to break their hurtful patterns. There is hope for any couple who decides to open up, say the hard truths and receive the help God gives through Christian community.

We are hopeful for ourselves and for many other couples on account of the great hope we have in Christ. Thanks to all the Christians Jim and I have known, thanks to everyone who's helping us now, and thanks especially to Jesus Christ the head of the church, we are making progress. We are different than we were twelve years ago. We're different than we were last month! Our prayer is that our progress will be evident to all, and that it will be contagious and inspiring.

Though every couple's story is unique, those of us in Christ are part of a bigger story we all share. God himself is conforming us to the image of his Son. There is hope for every couple in Christ.

Oh, that married couples who truly love the Lord would choose to be more married each day: More loving and respectful. More submissive and sacrificial. More careful in the boundaries we set. More genuinely *for* each other. More willing to follow the steps of confrontation and restoration. More humble in our expectations. More honest in owning up to our personal issues. More Christ-centered in our marriage. More willing to open up to other Christians.

The opportunity before us is significant. As we "become one flesh," married couples in Christ's body can together show the world the "great mystery" *(mega mystērion)* of marriage and thereby tell the story of the head and body union of Christ and his bride, the church.

ACKNOWLEDGMENTS

To begin with, we would like to thank our publisher for sponsoring this book. Special thanks are in order for Dave Zimmerman, our editor, for his competence. We hope to work with Dave someday again.

Second, we want to thank Larry Girard for inviting us to speak at Quaker Mountain near Porterville, California. That conference marked our first time to speak together on marriage. To make a long story short, during the last session things didn't go too well. Providentially, however, that now-hilarious episode led the whole retreat to by far the best discussion time of the weekend. When the next morning my (Sarah's) mind was exploding with ideas, I asked Jim if he would drive the eight-thousand-foot descent so that I could write a book proposal on marriage. I typed for three or four hours as Jim drove. Instead of going straight home, we took the exit to my office, so that I could duck inside and email the proposal to the publisher.

When a few months later I heard back from IVP that "yes" they wanted the book, I responded, "What book?" I had forgotten that I wrote it. But the project was meant to be. Thanks to Larry and Sue Girard who took an early chance on Jim and me.

Third, we want to thank John and Kathy Burke for writing the foreword and also for participating in our wedding. Their sacrificial gifts of singing, speaking and writing are appreciated.

Next, we want to thank Daniel Eichelberger, Kimberley Wiedefeld, Greg and Julie Nettle, Katie Loovis, and Chaplain Whiz Broome, who read the manuscript early and offered valuable feedback. We also thank the hundred-plus people—they know who they are—who gave us honest input that helped secure the title of this book.

From the depths of our heart, we especially want to thank every person who has prayed for our marriage. Those prayers have made a difference. In addition, we thank the people who have helped us gain perspective. We are indebted to many: To Chris and Sue from our engagement class at Willow

Creek Community Church whose last name we don't remember but whose influence on our life is still felt. To family members such as John Frank Chambers, who has counseled us as a brother by the hour; to John Stanley Chambers, who has helped us to relax; to Becky Chambers Hughes, whose encouragement has been priceless; to Debbie Draper, whose validation has been healing. To Sandy Miller who seems like family and whose thoughtful consolation can always spark a laugh.

We're also thankful for Lynn Irvin, who introduced us at Willow Creek; for our friends Peter and Angela Smith in Hereford, England, who believed in us as a couple at a time when we might have appeared to be mismatched; for Roy Wheeler, who supported us in our engagement and flew to Chicago from Texas at his own expense so that he could officiate our wedding, despite the fact that he had lost his voice; for Tom Jensen at Willow Creek, who helped us put into practice Matthew 18; for Nancy Grisham, who uniquely is both a "Jonathan" and a "Nathan" when it comes to being a friend; for other friends as well, such as La Verne Tolbert, Kara Powell, Ardath Smith, Wade Wollin, and Roger and Theresa White, who all pointed us to God.

We also want to acknowledge Don and Becky Durben, Tim and Patricia Lentz, Tim and Lisa Ferguson, Dan and Myra Perrine, and Ray and Janice Wheeler, all couples from New Song Church in San Dimas, California, with whom we have experienced authentic Christian community. Their honesty about their own marriages has strengthened not only us but also the book.

Thanks also to our church friends from Chicago: John and Susan Forbes, Bryan and Debbie Mangurten, Joel and Laurel Lehman, and Patrick and Kelly McNerney. The two who stand out most are Jim and Marianne Richter, who have supported us from day one with truth and grace. We are also grateful for Colin Smith, who preached a sermon during our engagement in Arlington Heights, Illinois, from which we drew the idea of making Ephesians 3:20—"rooted and grounded in love"—the lifelong theme of our marriage.

Our thanks would be incomplete without highlighting one more couple, Ken and Jenny Hultgren, whose testimony in marriage far surpasses ours and who became our closest friends in California when we first moved here and we needed them.

In closing, we want to thank Rick Puls, a wise and gentle counselor who has helped us probably more than any person.

Above all, we thank Jesus Christ who alone has made it possible for us to become true partners in forgiveness.

NOTES

Introduction: Becoming One Flesh

[1] Until God brought Eve to Adam, Adam had no concept of a woman, much les s marriage. One could go so far as to say that before God created Eve, Adam probably didn't realize he was a man. He probably didn't know he was a self. As Leon Kass suggests, "A solitary being, lacking a suitable mirror, might be incapable of self-knowledge." See Leon Kass, *The Beginning of Wisdom: Reading Genesis* (New York: Free Press, 2003), p.73.

[2] Animals can't get married because they live by instincts as opposed to moral choices. Thus animals do not marry; they mate. They can even stay with their mate for many years. Eagles, for instance, can live with the same mate for fifty years.

[3] On account of this common problem, the apostle Paul recommended that Christians who could handle it not even marry at all. In 1 Corinthians 7:32-35, Paul said, "One who is unmarried is concerned about the things of the Lord, ... but one who is married is concerned about the things of the world, how he may please his wife, and his interests are divided. The woman who is unmarried ... is concerned about the things of the Lord, that she may be holy both in body and spirit; but one who is married is concerned about the things of the world, how she may please her husband. This I say for your own benefit; not to put a restraint upon you, but to promote what is appropriate and to secure undistracted devotion to the Lord."

[4] For a more in-depth discussion, see "The Husband *Is* the Head," a chapter in Sarah's book *Men and Women in the Church* (Downers Grove, Ill.: InterVarsity Press, 2003), pp.154-72.

Chapter Two: Two Popular Models of Marriage

[1] See Colossians 1:26-27, for example, where the apostle Paul speaks of the *"mysterion* which has been hidden from the past ages and generations, but has now been manifested to His saints ... which is Christ in you, the hope of glory."

[2] See Eugene Peterson and Marva Dawn, *The Unnecessary Pastor* (Grand Rapids: Eerdmans, 2000), pp.70-71.

[3] According to my (Sarah's) doctoral professor, Wayne Grudem, the word kephalē never means "source" in the Greek translation of the Old Testament (called the Septuagint) and rarely, in his judgment, means "source" in ancient literature. Of the 2,336 examples of *kephalē* that Grudem researched from a wide range of ancient Greek literature, only 2 percent, in his judgment, ever appear to mean "person of

superior authority or rank, or ruler, or ruling part." Grudem's research is helpful because it alerts us to at least two important things: (1) one has to look outside of the New Testament to find examples of when kephalē connotes the idea of authority or source; (2) even outside of the New Testament, *kephalē* almost always refers unequivocally to the image of a physical head.

[4] An exception can be found in Acts 18:18. Here the word kephalē is translated as "hair" instead of "head." The Greek literally says, *"keiramenos ... tēn kephalēn."* That is, that Paul "shorn his head." Most English translations of Scripture render this Greek phrase with the words, "he had his hair cut."

[5] It is fundamentally wrong to say that women are more spiritual than men. It is also wrong to say that women are more *relational* than men. The triune nature of God reveals that God himself is relational in his essence. Since

both male and female are created in the image of God, both are innately relational. To state that men are less relational than women is to insinuate, quite falsely, that Jesus was relationally impaired merely by the fact that he was male. For more discussion on this, see Sarah Sumner, *Men and Women in the Church* (Downers Grove, Ill.: InterVarsity Press, 2003), pp.110-12.

[6] In early church history, it was the heretics who claimed that Mary was not a source of the Christ child. Orthodoxy argued that since Christ was born of God and woman, he is at once 100 percent divine and 100 percent human.

[7] Wayne Grudem and I together once lamented another problem—that so many have been mistaught to think that headship in the Bible refers to "covering." Countless Christians have been misled to wrongly think that the husband is the "covering" of the wife, and that the wife can only do certain things if her husband

is there to "cover" her. The big problem with this teaching is that *kephalē* does not mean "covering."
[8] "Behold, God is my *(ezer)* helper" (Psalm 54:4). See also Psalm 121:1; Isaiah 41:10.

Chapter Three: A Deeper Understanding of Headship

[1] Examples of metaphorical uses of kephalē include Ephesians 1:22; Colossians 2:10, 19, all of which suggest a picture of the union of a head and body.
[2] The full quote says this: "According to the Scriptures, the Father created the world, the Son created the world, and the Spirit created the world. The Father preserves all things, the Son upholds all things, and the Spirit is the source of life." These facts are expressed by saying that the persons of the Trinity concur in all external acts. See Charles Hodge, *Systematic Theology,* vol.1 (New York: Scribner, 1873), VI.2.A.5.

[3] Both husband and wife are powerless to save each other. They can edify each other. They can hold one another accountable. But they don't have the power to take charge of the other one's soul. No wife can save her husband. She can teach him how to pray; she can help him understand the gospel. But she cannot enliven his soul. The same can be said of the husband. No husband is responsible for his wife's discipleship. No husband can save his wife from sin and death. Both husband and wife must rely on Christ's salvation—for "there is salvation in one else" (Acts 4:12).

[4] A.T. Robertson, *Word Pictures in the New Testament,* vol.4 (Nashville: Broad man, 1931), p.545. See also T. K. Abbott, *A Critical and Exegetical Commentary on the Epistles to the Ephesians and to the Colossians* (Edinburgh: T & T Clark, 1909) p.166. Professor Abbott writes, "The apostle having compared the headship of the

husband to that of Christ, could not fail to think how imperfect the analogy was; he therefore emphatically calls attention to the point of difference; as if he would say: 'A man is the head of his wife, even as Christ also is the Head of the Church, although there is a vast difference, since He Himself is the Savior of the Body, of which He is Head; but notwithstanding this difference,' etc. Calvin already proposed this view."

[5] Leon Morris, Expository Reflections on the Book of Ephesians (Grand Rapids: Baker, 1994), p.187.

[6] It is true that an unbelieving spouse is "sanctified" through the believing spouse (See 1 Corinthians 7:14). But this passage is talking primarily about the spiritual status of children: "For the unbelieving husband is sanctified through his wife, and the unbelieving wife is sanctified through her believing husband; for otherwise your children are unclean, but now they are holy."

What we can learn additionally from this passage is that it is not unique to husbands—and thus not unique to headship—to sanctify the spouse.

Chapter Four: A Biblical Model of Marriage

[1] Perhaps the most famous example of an omission of the man's call to sacrifice can be found in *The Baptist Faith and Message,* adopted by the Southern Baptist Convention on June 14, 2000, and adopted or adapted into other large Christian ministries. I (Sarah) first read about in the *Los Angeles Times.* The statement says, "A wife is to submit herself graciously to the servant leadership of her husband." It says nothing about the husband sacrificing himself for his wife. This omission is significant insofar as it has led countless Christian couples to believe the headship of the husband *exempts* him from loving his wife in a self-sacrificial

way. Consider the further lines, "The husband and wife are of equal worth before God," and "[the husband] has the God-given responsibility to provide for, to protect, and to lead his family." The wife is "to serve as his helper in managing the household and nurturing the next generation" <www.sbc.net/bfm/bfm2000.asp#xviii>.

[2] For a great illustration of an intelligent wife who respected her foolish husband, see the story of Abigail and Nabal in 1 Samuel 25.

[3] See Eugene Peterson and Marva Dawn, *The Unnecessary Pastor* (Grand Rapids: Eerdmans, 2000), p.68.

[4] It's important to clarify that the Bible does *not* say that God hates people who have been divorced. God hates the sins that lead people to divorce, and God hates divorce itself, but God does not hate divorcees. Due to human hardness of heart, God allows for divorce in cases of sexual infidelity

and desertion by an unbelieving spouse.

[5] See David Gushee, *Getting Marriage Right* (Grand Rapids: Baker, 2004), p.61.

[6] See William Barclay, *The Gospel of Matthew,* vol. 2 (Philadelphia: Westminster Press, 1975), p.200. For further commentary on Jesus' teaching on divorce, see Sarah Sumner, Men and Women in the Church (Downers Grove, Ill.: InterVarsity Press, 2003), pp.164-67.

[7] The word for "joined together" in Greek is *synezeuxen,* and it means to be "yoked together." Grammatically *synezeuxen* appears as an aorist indicative, which connotes the idea of timelessness, in this case of a timeless union (though one that would cease upon the occasion of death).

Chapter Five: Practicing Oneness in the Grind of Daily Living

[1] Sexuality is an important aspect of marriage that we do not address much in this book. On the subject of sex in marriage, we recommend other books such as Mike Mason, The Mystery of Marriage (Portland, Ore.: Multnomah, 1985), and Ed Wheat, M.D., and Gaye Wheat, *Intended for Pleasure: Sex Technique and Sexual Fulfillment in Christian Marriage* (Grand Rapids: Revell, 1977).

[2] See John Hartley, *Genesis,* New International Biblical Commentary (Peabody, Mass.: Hendrickson, 2000), p.64. Hartley further says, "The focus is not on the resulting sexual relationship [of the new couple], or on the children to be born, though it does not exclude these expressions of their union. Rather ... in becoming one flesh a man and a woman become

more closely bonded [my emphasis] than their blood kinship.... Because the deepest human relationship is found in marriage, any spouse's abuse or domination of the other denies their mutuality and disrupts the harmony God intended."

[3] We also believe in practicing the disciplines that allow us to enjoy such freedom. If one of us starts to drift for instance, we practice the spiritual discipline of confession. Since Jim and I confess regularly, we are safeguarded by habit from hiding from each other. For sure, the warning is relevant: "Therefore let him who thinks he stands take heed that he does not fall" (1 Corinthians 10:12). The one who practices spiritual disciplines, however, is one who knows that he (or she) does *not* stand apart from the help of God. That's why they do the disciplines.

[4] C.S. Lewis, *The Four Loves* (New York: Harcourt, Brace, 1960), p.98.

[5] Ibid, p.103.
[6] Ibid.
[7] Ibid, p.91.
[8] Ibid, p.105.
[9] Leon J. Podles, The Church Impotent: The Feminization of Christianity (Dallas: Spence, 1999), pp.40, 45.
[10] A sacrifice-submit dynamic is illustrated in the sexual union of husband and wife. Whereas the husband is to sacrifice his immediate pleasure in order to bring his wife to a climax, so the wife must submit herself fully in order to reach the climax of her pleasure.
[11] First Corinthians 11:3 says, "I want you to understand that ... the man is the head of a woman." This line in Scripture reveals the essential oneness of all people. Male and female are inevitably connected. It was not good for the man to be alone in the Garden of Eden precisely because there was no woman. Men and women need each

other—to procreate, to coparent and to corule.

Chapter Six: Resolving Conflict

[1] A great book to read on marital forbearance is Jud Wilhite's *A Crazy Little Thing Called Love* (Cinncinnati, Ohio: Standard, 2007). I (Sarah) died laughing five or six times reading that book, especially when Jud tells the story of a husband who stockpiled a bag full of empty toilet paper rolls to prove to his wife that *he* replenished their toilet paper far more often than she did. The husband was so determined to win the argument that he literally dated the cardboard rolls with an ink pen and hid them in the closet in preparation for their next round of war.

[2] I (Sarah) am indebted to Tom Jensen at Willow Creek Community Church for guiding me through this process in 1995. Ever since

Tom coached me, my life has never been the same.

[3] We recommend professional Christian counseling for couples who need specialized help. Early in our marriage, we needed that kind of help, along with the help we also received from Christian friends.

Chapter Eight: Hot Button Issues

[1] C.S. Lewis says it's Christian and holy to joke about sex. See C.S. Lewis, *The Four Loves* (New York: Harcourt, Brace, 1960).
[2] This ridiculous fight illustrates my intuitive way of thinking (in general categories such as "shoes"), and Jim's sensory way of thinking (in specific categories such as "boots").

Chapter Nine: Building a Christ-Centered Marriage

[1] The book includes a workbook and a People Model Test that you can

take for finding out your primary type. See Sarah Sumner, *Leaderhsip Above the Line* (Carol Stream, Ill.: Tyndale House, 2006).

BACK COVER MATERIAL

As Sarah and Jim Sumner sought God together in the evangelism ministry of their church, their mutual admiration slowly turned to love, and the two were married. Just how married they're becoming is the story of this book.

Read *Just How Married Do You Want to Be?* and discover a fresh vision for how couples can become "one fl esh" in a marriage that honors God.

"Theological depth, and ... a great and timely teaching tool for changing the way people think about marriage, Christ and the church."

Chuck Colson, founder, Prison Fellowship

"Perhaps the most honest marriage book we have ever read—an honesty born of the real-life pain and struggle of two people with very different backgrounds and personalities.... Here is a marriage book without syrupy formulas or platitudes that tells us the truth that Jesus works through flawed vessels to create something beautiful."

Frank James, president, Reformed Theological Seminary—Orlando, and *Carolyn James,* author of *The Gospel of Ruth*

"Profound biblical theology that is incredibly practical. We believe you will find this book to be an enjoyable read that has the potential to change your marriage."

Greg Nettle, senior pastor, and **Julie Nettle,** worship leader, Rivertree Christian Church, Massillon, Ohio

"Matching faithful, Christ-centered scriptural exposition with honest, down-to-earth sharing, the Sumners show how marriage minus role-play becomes relationally real. This is a truly health-giving read."

J.I. Packer, author, *Knowing God*

JIM SUMNER is on the staff of NewSong Church in San Dimas, California.

SARA HSUMNER (Ph.D., Trinity Evangelical Divinity School) is the author of *Men and Women in the Church.*

www.ingramcontent.com/pod-product-compliance
Lightning Source LLC
Chambersburg PA
CBHW060555230426
43670CB00011B/1827